STAND OUT

Evidence-Based Learning for College and Career Readiness

5

THIRD EDITION

WORKBOOK

STACI JOHNSON

ROB JENKINS

D1568396

Australia • Brazil • Mexico • Singapore • United Kingdom • United States

**Stand Out 5: Evidence-Based Learning
for College and Career Readiness,
Third Edition**
Staci Johnson and Rob Jenkins
Workbook

Publisher: Sherrise Roehr

Executive Editor: Sarah Kenney

Development Editor: Lewis Thompson

Assistant Editor: Patricia Giunta

Director of Global Marketing: Ian Martin

Executive Marketing Manager: Ben Rivera

Product Marketing Manager: Dalia Bravo

Media Researcher: Leila Hishmeh

Director of Content and Media Production:
   Michael Burggren

Production Manager: Daisy Sosa

Senior Print Buyer: Mary Beth Hennebury

Cover and Interior Designer:
   Brenda Carmichael

Composition: Lumina

Cover Image: Seth Joel/Getty Images

Bottom Images: Jay B Sauceda/Getty Images;
   Tripod/Getty Images; Portra Images/Getty
   Images; Portra Images/Getty Images; Mark
   Edward Atkinson/Tracey Lee/Getty Images;
   Hero Images/Getty Images; Jade/Getty
   Images; James Porter/Getty Images; LWA/
   Larry Williams/Getty Images; Dimitri Otis/
   Getty Images

For permission to use material from this text or product,
submit all requests online at **cengage.com/permissions**
Further permissions questions can be emailed to
permissionrequest@cengage.com

Work Book
ISBN 13: 978-1-305-65566-9

National Geographic Learning/Cengage Learning
20 Channel Center Street
Boston, MA 02210
USA

Cengage Learning is a leading provider of customized learning solutions with office locations around the globe, including Singapore, the United Kingdom, Australia, Mexico, Brazil and Japan. Locate our local office at:
international.cengage.com/region

Visit National Geographic Learning online at **NGL.Cengage.com**
Visit our corporate website at **www.cengage.com**

Printed at CLDPC, USA, 11-22

CONTENTS

TO THE TEACHER

ABOUT THE SERIES

The **Stand Out** series is designed to facilitate *active* learning within life-skill settings that leads students to career and academic pathways. Each student book and its supplemental components in the six-level series expose students to competency areas most useful and essential for newcomers, with careful treatment of level-appropriate but challenging materials. Students grow academically by developing essential literacy and critical thinking skills that will help them find personal success in a changing and dynamic world.

STAND OUT WORKBOOK

The **Stand Out Workbook** is designed to provide additional practice for learners to reinforce what they learned in each student book lesson. It can be used as homework or as a supplement to the lesson in the classroom. Each lesson in **Stand Out** is driven by a life-skill objective and supported by vocabulary and grammar. Students are not expected to master or acquire vocabulary and grammar completely after being exposed to it just one time, hence the need for additional practice. The lessons in the student book are three pages long and each supporting workbook lesson is also three pages long. The workbook lessons correlate directly with the student book lessons.

The **Stand Out Workbook** establishes a link to new content by providing the essential vocabulary introduced in the books in a way that also promotes critical thinking skills. Promoting critical thinking skills is essential for students to become independent lifelong learners. About half of the three-page practice is grammar focused where students are given a chart with notes, study how the grammar facilitates communication, and gain additional needed confidence through practice.

HOW TO USE THE STAND OUT WORKBOOK

The workbook can be used in the following ways:

1. The activities in the workbook can be used as additional practice during class to reinforce one or more practice activities in the student book.

2. The activities in the workbook can be assigned as homework. This is often a good way to reinforce what students have learned. The skills, vocabulary, and structures may not transfer into long-term memory after the lesson, so reinforcing the lesson after a short period of time away can be very helpful. Additionally, teachers can also review the homework at the beginning of each class, giving students another opportunity to be exposed to the information. Reviewing the homework is also a good strategy for the *Warm-up/Review* portion of the lesson and can be used in place of the one proposed in the **Stand Out Lesson Planner**.

3. The **Stand Out Workbook** can be used as a tool in the flipped classroom. In flipped classrooms, students prepare for lessons away from class before they are presented. Since the **Stand Out Workbook** introduces much of the vocabulary and grammar for each lesson, it is ideal for incorporating this approach.

ADDITIONAL PRACTICE

The **Stand Out** series is a comprehensive one-stop resource for all student needs. There is no need to look any further than the resources offered. Additional practice is available through the online workbook, which is different from the print workbook. There are also hundreds of multi-level worksheets available online. Please visit ngl.cengage.com/so3 to get easy access to all resources.

LESSON **1** Classroom community

GOAL ■ Get to know people

A. Imagine you know the people below. Write notes about them. Use your imagination!

| **Kenji** | **Anya** | **Gilberto** | **Marie** |

Kenji: _____

Anya: _____

Gilberto: _____

Marie: _____

B. Write a description for each person based on the notes you wrote in Exercise A.

EXAMPLE: Kenji is a happy person. He is a student from Japan. He likes to play basketball.

Kenji: _____

_____

Anya: _____

_____

Gilberto: _____

_____

Marie: _____

_____

C. **Study the chart.**

Introductions	
Introduction	**Responding to an introduction**
I'd like to introduce you to Juan. I'd like you to meet Peter. This is my friend, Ana. Do you know Caroline? Have you met my brother, Zach?	It's a pleasure to meet you. It's a pleasure meeting you. (I'm) pleased to meet you. (It's) nice to meet you. (It's) good to meet you.
In short common introductions with phrases and statements, it is appropriate in speaking to leave off the subject and the verb. The subject and verb are implied.	

D. **Write a response to each introduction. Use a different expression for each one.**

1. **Student A:** I'd like to introduce you to my friend, Maddy.

   Student B: _It's nice to meet you, Maddy._

2. **Student A:** Do you know Erin?

   Student B: _____

3. **Student A:** Have you met Chinh?

   Student B: _____

4. **Student A:** I'd like you to meet Enrique.

   Student B: _____

5. **Student A:** This is my sister, Cristina.

   Student B: _____

6. **Student A:** I'd like to introduce you to Mrs. Pino.

   Student B: _____

E. **Study the chart.**

Simple Past/Present Perfect/Simple Present		
Simple past	Something that started and ended in the past.	Juan was born in 1989.
Present perfect	Something that started in the past and continues in the present.	Juan has been in the United States for three years.
Present	Something that is true about the present.	Juan works in a department store.
Future	Something that will happen in the future.	Juan is going to / will study architecture in college.

F. **Complete the sentences about each of the people using the verbs and tenses listed in parentheses.**

1. Chinh _____ is _____ (be – present) a student.

2. He _____ (live – present) in Texas now.

3. He _____ (move – future) to California in a few months.

4. Chinh _____ (come – past) from Vietnam five years ago.

5. Chinh _____ (be – present perfect) in school for two years.

6. She _____ (study – future) nursing once her English improves.

7. Enrique _____ (be – past) an engineer in Mexico.

8. He _____ (move – present perfect) three times since he came to the U.S.

9. He _____ (like – present) to see new places and meet new people.

10. He _____ (keep – future) moving so he can find an engineering job.

G. **Zhou is introducing you to his friend Erin. Complete the conversation with appropriate phrases.**

Zhou: I'd like you to meet my friend, Erin.

You: _____

Erin: What's your name?

You: _____

Erin: I'm actually from here, but I was born in Sweden. Where were you born?

You: _____

Erin: I came here 15 years ago with my family. What about you?

You: _____

Erin: How interesting. It's so nice to have met you. I hope we see each other in school.

LESSON **2** **What are your hobbies?**

GOAL ■ Talk about personal interests

A. Write four things you think the people below are interested in doing.

Name: Amelia
Interests:

1. _____
2. _____
3. _____
4. _____

Name: Klara
Interests:

1. _____
2. _____
3. _____
4. _____

Name: Oscar
Interests:

1. _____
2. _____
3. _____
4. _____

Name: Ana
Interests:

1. _____
2. _____
3. _____
4. _____

B. Look at what you wrote in Exercise A. Circle the person you are most like.

C. Study the chart.

Asking about personal interests	Responses
So, what do you like to do in your free time? What are your hobbies? What are your interests outside of school/work? Are you into music? What do you like to do? What are your plans for the weekend? What's your favorite movie?	That's interesting. How fun! Wow, that's great. Me, too! Not me. I . . . Sounds like we have something in common.

Conversations are more productive when . . .
   you ask about the person you are talking to.
   you take interest in the person you are talking to.
   you ask follow-up questions.
Other strategies:
   Learn to summarize what someone says when you don't understand.
   Learn to disagree politely, showing respect for the other person's opinion.
   Learn to express yourself clearly and in a simple way.
   Learn to maintain eye contact.

D. Circle the best answer to each question.

1. **Q:** So, what do you like to do in your free time?

   A: I like to go to the movies. / No, not much.

2. **Q:** What are your hobbies?

   A: Reading books and fixing up old cars. / We're going to the mountains.

3. **Q:** What are your interests outside of school/work?

   A: I'm a carpenter. / Playing soccer and cooking.

4. **Q:** What do you like to do?

   A: I like fresh fruit and red meat. / I like to train for bike races.

5. **Q:** What are your plans for the weekend?

   A: Surfing and reading comic books. / I'm going to a family reunion.

E. Complete the conversation with the responses below.

a. I like to ride my bike.

b. Yes, I'm usually training for bike races.

c. I like to have fun while I'm exercising.

d. I think it's exciting and healthy, too. It's a also a great way to meet people.

1. **Student A:** What do you like to do in your free time?

   Student B: _____

2. **Student A:** Why do you sing when you exercise?

   Student B: _____

3. **Student A:** I've heard that hiking is both exciting and healthy. What do you think?

   Student B: _____

4. **Student A:** Is it true that you spend a lot of time riding your bike?

   Student B: _____

F. Answer the following questions about yourself.

1. What do you like to do in your free time?

   _____

   _____

2. What sports are you into?

   _____

   _____

3. What are your plans for the weekend?

   _____

   _____

4. What's your favorite type of music?

   _____

   _____

LESSON **3** Dear friend

GOAL ■ Write a personal message

A. Answer the following questions.

1. Do you write personal, handwritten letters? If so, to whom?

_____

_____

2. Do you write personal e-mails? If so, to whom?

_____

_____

3. Do you prefer to write personal, handwritten letters or e-mails? Why?

_____

_____

B. There are eight mistakes in Andrea's letter. Circle each mistake you find.

Dear Alexi,

I'm so anxious to see you. I can't wait for your visit in july. We are going having a great time. I want to show you my new school. we learning a lot of interesting things right now. My english is improving. This school private is great! I'm preparing for work in the business feild. I will meet you at the bus stop at four o'clock on monday.

Your friend always,

Andrea

C. Study the chart.

Editing	
Capitalization	Capitalize every proper noun. Capitalize the first letter of the first word of every new sentence.
Spelling	Check spelling in a dictionary or ask a friend.
Nouns	Check to make sure nouns are written correctly (singular or plural).
Verbs	Verbs should agree with the noun and be in the correct tense.
Word order	Make sure subjects in statements come before the verb and that adjectives come before the noun they describe.
Punctuation	Every sentence should end with a period, exclamation point, or question mark. Separate series (three or more adjectives or nouns) with commas.

D. Look back at the letter you corrected in Exercise B. Decide which types of mistakes you corrected.

Corrected Mistake   Type of Mistake

1. __July_____   _capitalization_____

2. _____   _____

3. _____   _____

4. _____   _____

5. _____   _____

6. _____   _____

7. _____   _____

8. _____   _____

E. Underline the correct sentences. Edit the incorrect sentences. On the lines, write the types of mistakes using the terms from the chart in Exercise C.

1. <u>Last Monday, I registered for classes at my new school.</u>

   l̲ast m̲onday, I registered for classes at my new school. _____ capitalization _____

2. The bookstore sell books for all the classes.

   The bookstore sells books for all the classes. _____

3. Have you ever been to the art museum on campus.

   Have you ever been to the art museum on campus? _____

4. No, but I did go to the local exhibit art that came to town.

   No, but I did go to the local art exhibit that came to town. _____

5. Last week, she met with the guidance counselor.

   Last week, she met with the giudance counslor. _____

6. The counselor told her that she should take some harder class.

   The counselor told her that she should take some harder classes. _____

F. Correct the mistakes in each sentence. Some sentences have more than one mistake.

1. Chinh looked at many ~~school~~ schools before she chose the best one for nursing.

2. she was looking for one with the best teachers?

3. She got great recomenations from the teachers at her previus school.

4. She hope to complete her degree in three yeas.

5. She is going to moves so she can be closer to her new school

6. chinh will have to work at night so she can pays for school.

7. She have a time-part job as a server food in a restaurant.

G. Imagine you are Chinh writing a letter to Jason, a friend you met at your last school. Write a personal letter on a separate piece of paper. Include all of the information from Exercise F.

LESSON **1** Learning styles

GOAL ■ Identify learning styles

A. Read the paragraphs. Describe the learners using the learning styles in the box.

visual/spatial	verbal/linguistic	~~logical/mathematical~~
body/kinesthetic	musical/rhythmic	

1. Marion likes to make connections between what she has heard before and what she is learning at the moment. She often tries to put things in categories. She analyzes all the information before she completely understands new concepts. Marion is a
_____logical/mathematical_____ learner.

2. Neda is always singing. Sometimes the teacher asks her to sing to herself because she can start singing very loudly and does not even know it. She tries to be quieter, but then she begins to tap out rhythms on her desk with her fingers. Neda is a
_____ learner.

3. Mario needs to see what he is learning. Listening to information is not enough. When he listens to teachers or finds out about new information, he tries to draw it out. He often makes graphs and charts to understand something better. Mario is a
_____ learner.

4. Cynthia likes to discuss new information with her friend in class. She often repeats what the instructor says to her friend. When she does this, she understands it much better.
Cynthia is a _____ learner.

5. Jim and John are always interested in moving around in the room. They do not mind changing positions and trying to act out what is being discussed. Jim and John are
_____ learners.

B. Write a short paragraph about your own learning style. Use the paragraphs in Exercise A as a model.

_____

_____

_____

_____

_____

C. Study the chart.

Gerunds as Objects of Prepositions			
Verb	**Prep.**	**Gerund**	**Example sentence**
learn learn best	by	writing participating listening repeating watching relating solving remembering taking identifying	He **learns by writing** everything down. They **learn best by participating** in a discussion.
learn	through		They **learn through listening**.
practice	by		We **practice by repeating** what we hear. I **practice by watching** a video.
(be) good	at		Logical learners **are good at solving** problems.
excel succeed	in		You **excel in remembering** information. I **succeed in taking** good notes.
struggle	with		That student **struggles with identifying** main ideas.

D. Complete the sentences with the correct forms of the verbs in parentheses.

1. Mehry _____learns_____ (learn) best by _____taking_____ (take) detailed notes.

2. I always _____ (struggle) with _____ (solve) math problems.

3. They _____ (be) really good at _____ (remember) what they've heard.

4. His teacher _____ (excel) at _____ (explain) ideas clearly.

5. Peter _____ (practice) by _____ (repeat) facts out loud.

6. Kim and her study partner _____ (learn) by _____ (participate).

7. He _____ (be) not good at _____ (relate) to other students.

8. They _____ (learn) best by _____ (work) together.

9. She always _____ (succeed) in _____ (create) projects.

E. Circle the correct preposition.

1. She practices (in / **by**) drawing pictures.

2. He succeeds (in / with) remembering obscure facts.

3. They struggle (by / with) taking clear notes.

4. She learns (by / at) memorizing the notes she has taken.

5. Therese is good (in / at) identifying scientific solutions.

6. I practice math (by / with) solving five problems every night.

7. My brother succeeds (at / in) memorizing mathematical equations.

F. Look back at the people in Exercise A. Write a sentence to describe each person using gerunds as objects of prepositions. Use a different verb and gerund for each statement you write.

1. Marion _practices by putting things in categories_____.

2. Neda _____.

3. Mario _____.

4. Cynthia _____.

5. Jim and John _____.

G. Write about your learning style. Use gerunds as objects of prepositions.

1. I struggle with _memorizing new concepts_____.

2. I excel at _____.

3. _____ finishing my homework quickly.

4. I struggle _____.

5. _____ taking detailed notes.

6. _____

7. _____

LESSON ② Career planning

GOAL ■ Identify career paths

A. Define the different educational qualifications. Then, write how long it takes to earn each one?

High school diploma or GED certificate

What: _____ Time: _____

Associate of Arts degree (AA)

What: _____ Time: _____

Bachelor's degree (BA or BS)

What: _____ Time: _____

Master's degree (MA or MS)

What: _____ Time: _____

Doctorate (PhD)

What: _____ Time: _____

B. Look at the list of jobs below. What level of education is needed for each one?

Job or career	Level of education needed
architect	
farmer	
firefighter	
computer engineer	
professional soccer player	
teacher	
musician	
salesperson	
small business owner	
food server	
lawyer	
dentist	
journalist	

C. Study the chart.

Future Conditional Statements		
If clause (condition) *if* + subject + present tense verb	Future statement (result) subject + *will* + base verb	Example sentence
if she gets a master's degree	she will make more money	**If** she gets a master's degree, she will make more money. She will make more money **if** she gets a master's degree.
if he is good at computations	he will do well with computers	**If** he is good at computations, he will do well with computers. He will do well with computers **if** he is good at computations.
The future statement is dependent on whether or not the *if* clause happens or not. The *if* clause cannot stand alone. The *if* clause can come first or second. When the *if* clause comes first, use a comma. When the *if* clause follows the future statement, don't use a comma.		

D. Circle the condition and underline the result in each sentence.

1. I will go to school full-time if I save up enough money.

2. If she passes the bar exam, she will practice law in Texas.

3. I will look for a job as a dental assistant if I get my certificate.

4. If Emil doesn't get into the university, he will go to a community college and then transfer.

5. If she wants to be a doctor, she will have to go to medical school.

6. He will have to look for investors if he wants to start his own business.

7. If Sasha gets an internship at that company, they will pay for her to go to school.

8. Brian will pass his finals if he studies hard.

E. Correct each statement below.

1. If Maya ~~go~~ *goes* to technical school, she will get a better job.

2. Mario will have to get another job if he want to pay for college.

3. If Elias moves out of the city, he will finding better job opportunities.

4. If we finished our degrees in three years, we can start working sooner.

5. Kendra will application to several more schools if she doesn't get into her first choice.

6. She will ask her boss to change her hours if she get accepted at the technical school.

7. Will you apply for scholarships if you went to the university?

F. Complete each statement with a condition or a result.

1. If I don't pass the entrance exam, _I will study harder and take it again_____.

2. If I get into college, _____.

3. I will get a better job _____.

4. I will make more money _____.

5. If I quit my job, _____.

G. Complete the table with your career goals. Decide on a timeline.

	Career goal	Completion date
Goal 1		
Goal 2		
Goal 3		
Goal 4		

GOAL ■ Balance your life

A. Think about your roles.

1. What is a role? _____

2. How many roles do you have? _____

3. Make a list below:

   I am a(n) _____.

   I am a(n) _____.

   I am a(n) _____.

   I am a(n) _____.

   I am a(n) _____.

   I am a(n) _____.

4. Look at the list you made above. Which is your hardest role? Circle it.

B. Read about Andre.

I have a busy life. My family is the most important thing to me. My family is the reason I work a lot. I work so much because I need to make money so I can support them. I have to travel for my job every week, so I see my wife, two children, and dog only on the weekend. When I am home, I am tired so I sleep a lot. Before I had this job, I didn't travel and I worked from home. It was a good job, but I needed to make more money to pay for all our new expenses. When I get a promotion, I will work less. I will work from the office, which is only three miles from my house. I will work hard now so I can slow down in the future.

C. Answer the questions below.

1. What does Andre say is most important to him? Do you agree? What do you think his wife and children think?

   _____

2. Will Andre work fewer hours after he gets a promotion? Why?

   _____

D. Study the chart.

Simple Tenses				
Subject	Past	Present	Future	
I	spent	spend	will spend	more time with my brothers.
You	enjoyed	enjoy	will enjoy	being a mother.
He, She, It	studied	studies	will study	English every day.
We	put	put	will put	our studies first.
They	worked	work	will work	too many hours.

E. Complete each sentence with the correct form of the verb _study_.

1. Next year, I _____will study_____ math.

2. Last week, I _____ with a new partner.

3. Right now, he _____ at the library every day.

4. Next week, they _____ for their final exams.

5. She never _____ by herself these days.

6. Last year, George _____ science and math.

7. Next year, he _____ literature.

F. Complete each sentence with the correct form of the verb _work_.

1. In the past, we always _____ on weeknights.

2. Two years ago, I _____ over 50 hours a week.

3. Yesterday, he _____ a short shift.

4. Jessica _____ at night next week so she can be home with her kids during the day.

5. Next month, they _____ a lot of overtime.

6. Manjuri never _____ on Sundays nowadays.

G. Study the chart and complete each sentence with the correct form of the verb *be*.
More than one answer may be correct.

Be			
Subject	**Past**	**Present**	**Future**
I	was	am	will be
You	were	are	will be
He, She, It	was	is	will be
We	were	are	will be
They	were	are	will be

1. I _____ always trying to do better at my job.

2. She _____ still in school last year.

3. He _____ never late to English class.

4. Next month, I _____ taking a higher level class.

5. Keira and Isaac _____ always competing for the top spot in class last year.

6. You _____ late every day last week.

H. Complete the paragraph with an appropriate form of one of the verbs in the box.
Some verbs may be used more than once.

be	want	take	get	look	need	have

Right now, I _____ a student. I study history and political science. One day,

I _____ _____ a teacher and teach in high school, so

I _____ to get my special subjects teaching credentials. My classes

_____ really hard, and I _____ to study for at least three hours

every night. Last year, I _____ easier classes so I _____ able to

work and go to school at the same time. But this year, I _____ only going to

school. I _____ my bachelor's degree at the end of next year, and then

I _____ to take classes for my credentials. That _____ about

a year. Hopefully, I _____ able to pass the credential exams, and then I

_____ for a job as a teacher.

L E S S O N ④ Setting priorities

GOAL ■ Identify and prioritize goals

A. **Look at the events in Eva's life. Number the events from *1* to *9* in the order they most likely occurred.**

_____ She got a job as a waitress speaking English.

_____ She got a job with a local newspaper.

_____ She graduated from university.

___1__ She learned English at an adult school.

_____ She sold a book to a publisher.

_____ She studied journalism.

_____ She took classes at a community college.

_____ She went to university.

_____ She wrote a book of English poems.

B. **Write *true* or *false* in front of each statement based on your responses in Exercise A.**

1. _____ Eva had learned English before she got a job as a waitress.

2. _____ Before she went to a university, she had gone to a community college.

3. _____ After she had studied journalism, she wrote a book of English poems.

4. _____ She had gotten a job with a local newspaper before she graduated.

C. **Take the two statements that are false and rewrite them so they are true.**

1. _____

_____

2. _____

_____

D. **Study the chart.**

Past Perfect				
Subject	*Had/Hadn't*	**Past participle**	**Complement**	**Clause**
I, He, She, We, You, They	had hadn't	trained	for six months	before I ran the marathon.
		(already) taken	English classes	when he started college.
		studied	at the university	she went to medical school.*
*After **she had studied** at university, **she went** to medical school.				
The past perfect can show an event that happened before another event in the past. The past perfect can show that something happened before the verb in the *when* clause. *The past perfect can show something that happened after another event. In this case, the *after* clause includes the past perfect and the clauses are separated with a comma.				

E. **Underline what happened first.**

1. <u>After I had studied computer science,</u> I got a job as a programmer.

2. Gabe had worked as a mechanic before he went to technical school.

3. When I got my degree, I had already been teaching for five years.

4. Kevin learned how to use a computer after he had graduated from high school.

5. Before they applied to college, they had studied English for three years.

F. **Complete each sentence with the correct form of the verb.**

1. After she ___had started___ (start) her own cleaning business, she ___went___ (go) to business school.

2. Before you _____ (finish) school, you _____ (work) full-time as a photographer.

3. She _____ (study) at an adult school for four years before she

   _____ (apply) to college.

4. After Antonia _____ (find) a good school for her kids, she _____ (begin) to look for a school for herself.

5. Evan _____ already _____ (pick) a major when he

   _____ (register) for his first year of school.

G. Take one idea from the first column and another idea from the second column and write past perfect sentences.

~~get together a portfolio~~	apply for a job with a shipping company
ride four days a week	~~find an art school~~
work for the postal service	compete in a bicycle race
meet with a counselor	kids are born
save money for college	choose a college major

EXAMPLE: _I had gotten together a portfolio before I found an art school._

1. _____

2. _____

3. _____

4. _____

H. Think about a goal you have accomplished. Write the goal and the steps you took to achieve it.

GOAL: _____

Step 1: _____

Step 2: _____

Step 3: _____

Step 4: _____

Step 5: _____

Step 6: _____

I. Write two past perfect sentences describing your steps in Exercise H.

1. _____

2. _____

LESSON **5** Motivation

GOAL ■ Motivate yourself

A. **Read Felipe's goals below. Which ones do you share? Circle the ones you have in common.**

1. Learn English.

2. Graduate from college.

3. Get married.

4. Have children.

5. Get a job that pays over $50,000 a year.

6. Buy a new house.

B. **List some obstacles that might keep Felipe from reaching the goals above.**

1. _____

2. _____

3. _____

C. **Come up with a list of ways to help Felipe stay motivated to reach his goals.**

1. _____

2. _____

3. _____

4. _____

5. _____

6. _____

D. **Study the chart.**

Future Perfect Tense				
Subject	*Will have*	Past participle		Second future event (present tense)
I	will have	become	a teacher	by the time my kids are in school.
He	will have	been	a graphic designer (for five years)	when he turns 35.
They	will have	found	a job	by the time they finish school.
We use the future perfect to talk about an activity that will be completed before another time or event in the future. Note: The order of events is not important. If the second future event comes first, use a comma. *By the time my kids are in school, I will have become a teacher.*				

E. **Match the goals with the time periods and write complete sentences below.**

1. Sharon and Vu will have started their business

2. Sharon will have hired all the employees

3. Vu will have completed construction

4. They will have been open for six months

a. by the end of the month.

b. when they turn 40.

c. when their kids graduate from high school.

d. by the time the doors open.

1. Sharon and Vu will have started their business when they turn 40.

2. _____

3. _____

4. _____

F. Complete each sentence with the correct future perfect form of the words in parentheses.

1. By the time school _____starts_____ (start), Franco __will have chosen__ (choose) a major.

2. He _____ (give) his notice at work before the first day of class _____ (begin).

3. Greta _____ (buy) a new computer before her first paper _____ (be) due.

4. By the time he _____ (complete) his first marathon, he _____ (run) over 250 miles.

5. When she _____ (turn) 50, she _____ (married) for over 25 years.

6. You _____ (look) at 15 schools by the time you finally _____ (choose) one.

7. His father _____ (get) his high school diploma when his son _____ (graduate) from college.

G. Use the future perfect form to complete each of the statements below.

1. By the time I have my degree, _I will have studied for more than eight years_____.

2. By the time I get home, _____.

3. When I graduate from college, _____.

4. When I turn 70, _____.

5. When my English is perfect, _____.

6. By 2025, _____.

7. By the time I reach my goal, _____.

PRACTICE TEST

A. Read and circle the best answers.

Do you learn best through seeing? Then you are a visual learner. Visual learners learn from body language and facial expressions. They like to sit in the front of the classroom so they can see clearly. They tend to think in pictures and learn best by looking at visuals, such as diagrams, pictures, videos, and handouts. Visual learners like to take detailed notes to help learn information.

Do you learn best by listening? Then you are an auditory learner. Auditory learners learn best by listening to lectures, participating in discussions, and listening to what others say. They also listen to tone of voice, pitch, and speed to interpret hidden meanings. Auditory learners learn best if they read text aloud.

Do you like to learn by moving, doing, and touching? Then you are a tactile or kinesthetic learner. Kinesthetic learners like to actively explore their surroundings by touching things and moving. They have trouble sitting still for long periods of time. They learn best through a hands-on approach.

1. What are the three types of learners mentioned in the reading?
   a. visual, tactile, kinesthetic
   b. auditory, visual, kinesthetic
   c. seeing, listening, touching
   d. none of the above

2. Which type of leaner thinks in pictures?
   a. tactile
   b. visual
   c. kinesthetic
   d. auditory

3. Which of the following does NOT describe a kinesthetic learner?
   a. likes to touch things
   b. participates in discussions
   c. explores by moving
   d. sometimes has trouble sitting still

4. Which two types of learners are the same?
   a. visual and auditory
   b. auditory and tactile
   c. kinesthetic and tactile
   d. visual and kinesthetic

LESSON ① Getting organized

GOAL ■ Organize finances

A. Tuba is 22 years old and depends on her parents to help her financially. She has a high school diploma and is making plans. Read about her goals.

> I have many goals that are very important to me. First of all, I want to become financially independent. But before I do that, I need to pay off my credit cards. Right now, I work two jobs to pay rent on a small apartment downtown, and I have to pay $200 a month for the minimum balance on my credit cards. Unfortunately, I don't save any money. So, starting today, I will begin to save, and I will stop impulse buying. If I save $300 a month, I will have paid off my credit cards by the time I am 25. I also plan to pay off my car. I need a better job, so I'm going to improve my English and get a college degree. I'd like to become a nurse. By the time I turn 30, I will have a career and make a good living.

B. Predict how long it might take Tuba to reach her goals.

Goal	Length of Time
stop impulse buying	
pay off her credit cards	
pay off her car	
finish college and get a degree	
start a career	

C. What are some financial goals that you have and how long do you think it will take you to reach them?

Goal	Length of Time

D. **Study the chart.**

Future Perfect Tense	
Completed future event	**Second future event**
I will have saved $3,000	by the time he arrives.
You will have paid off the house	when you reach retirement.
They will have found a job	by the time they finish school.
We use the future perfect to talk about an activity that will be completed before another time or event in the future.	

Future activity	Length of time	Second future event
I will have been saving	for three years	by the time he arrives.
You will have been paying	for 30 years	when you reach retirement.
They will have been looking for a job	for four years	by the time they finish school.
We use the future perfect progressive to talk about an activity that will be completed before another time or event in the future. However, in future perfect progressive, the length of time is included.		
Note: Sometimes, either tense can be used and the meaning remains the same. For example: *I will have lived in the house for thirty years by the time I move.* **Or** *I will have been living in this house for thirty years by the time I move.*		

E. **Decide which sentence in each pair is the future perfect or the future perfect progressive. Write *FP* (future perfect) or *FPP* (future perfect progressive).**

1. __FP__ **A.** I will have searched long and hard for a financial planner before I find one.

   __FPP__ **B.** I will have been searching for a financial planner for six months by the time I find one.

2. _____ **A.** He will have saved $5,000 for a car by the time he turns 20.

   _____ **B.** He will have been saving for eight years by the time he turns 20.

3. _____ **A.** You will have been looking for a computer for six months before you buy one.

   _____ **B.** You will have looked all over for a computer before you buy one.

4. _____ **A.** She will have been managing the household finances for over 15 years before she finally gives them over to her husband.

   _____ **B.** She will have managed the household finances all by herself before she finally gives them over to her husband.

F. **Complete each sentence with the future perfect or the future perfect progressive.**

1. At the rate you're going, I _____will have finished_____ (finish) my lunch before you have made your menu selections.

2. We _____ (pay) off our cars by the time we need new ones.

3. He _____ (start) contributing to college accounts for his kids by the time they are born.

4. You _____ (plan) your retirement party for months by the time you actually retire.

5. They _____ (look) for a house for six years by the time they can afford one.

6. I _____ (spend) thousands of dollars by the time I finish school.

7. My sister _____ (have) ten jobs before she finds the one she is happy with.

G. **Look at the predictions you made for Tuba in Exercise B. Write sentences using the indicated verb tense.**

1. FP   Tuba will have stopped impulse buying in three months. _____

2. FPP   _____

3. FPP   _____

4. FP   _____

5. FPP   _____

H. **Now look back at the two goals you wrote for yourself in Exercise C and write sentences using either the future perfect or the future perfect progressive.**

1. _____

2. _____

LESSON ② Managing money

GOAL ■ Reduce debt and save money

A. Review the following vocabulary by coming up with a definition for each phrase in your own words.

1. impulse buying: _____

2. buying in bulk: _____

3. living paycheck to paycheck: _____

4. purchasing power: _____

5. living within your means: _____

6. liquid assets: _____

B. Look at Sheila and Sam's spending habits in the past and now. Circle the habits that have improved. Underline the habits that have gotten worse.

In the Past	Now
bought designer clothes	bargain shop
made coffee at home	buy coffee at a coffee shop
bought in bulk	buy things at the market when needed
spent every penny they made	have a savings account

C. Think about your own spending habits and complete the table below.

In the Past	Now
1.	1.
2.	2.
3.	3.
4.	4.

D. Study the chart.

Past Perfect Progressive Tense					
First past activity				**Second past event**	
Subject	**_Had_**	**_Been_**	**_-ing_ verb**		**Simple past**
Sheila	had	been	buying	designer clothes	before she started bargain shopping.
Sam	had	been	making	coffee at home	before he began buying it at a coffee shop.
They	had	been	paying	a higher deductible	before they called the insurance company.
We use the past perfect progressive to talk about an activity that was happening for a while before another event that happened in the past. For the more recent event, we use the simple past.					

E. Circle the most recent past activity. Underline the prior past event.

1. She <u>had been spending her tips</u> before she decided to save up for a computer.

2. We had been paying cash for everything until we got credit cards.

3. Before he had a bank account, he had been saving his money in a drawer.

4. Lisa had been paying her bills by check every month until she started banking online.

5. I had been spending my whole paycheck until I started saving for retirement.

F. Rewrite each sentence above, reversing the two events. Pay attention to comma placement.

1. _Before she decided to save up for a computer, she had been spending her tips._

2. _____

3. _____

4. _____

5. _____

G. Complete each sentence with the correct form of the past perfect progressive.

1. We _____had been living_____ (live) beyond our means before my wife lost her job.

2. Before Felipe rode his bike to work, he _____ (drive) an expensive car.

3. Margaret _____ (eat) dinner out every night before she started cooking at home.

4. My husband and I _____ (do) the finances together each month before I started doing them by myself.

5. Until you decided to lease a car, you _____ (make) payments to own your car.

6. We _____ (hire) babysitters a lot before we started taking the kids out with us.

7. Before the couple got married, they _____ (meet) with separate financial advisors.

H. Look back at Sheila and Sam's spending habits in Exercise B. Write sentences using the past perfect progressive.

1. _They had been buying designer clothes before they started shopping for bargains._

2. _____

3. _____

4. _____

I. Look back at your completed table in Exercise C. Write sentences about your own spending habits. Make sure you use the past perfect progressive.

1. _____

2. _____

3. _____

4. _____

LESSON ③ Investing wisely

GOAL ■ Identify investment strategies

A. Review the following vocabulary by matching each word or phrase to its correct definition.

1. value		a. a punishment by law
2. inflation		b. things readily converted into cash
3. penalty		c. possibility of danger
4. purchasing power		d. to change into another form
5. liquid assets		e. an increase in prices of goods and services
6. net appreciation		f. what something is worth
7. convert		g. ability to purchase based on income
8. risky		h. final increase after losses are accounted for

B. Write sentences with two of the words in Exercise A.

1. _____

2. _____

C. Check (✓) the things you *can* do.

1. _____ save money

2. _____ get a better job

3. _____ balance a checkbook

4. _____ pay bills online

5. _____ apply for a credit card

6. _____ invest in the stock market

D. Choose one of the things you can do in Exercise C. On a separate piece of paper, write what you need in order to be able to do it.

EXAMPLE: *In order to save money, I need to have a job that pays me money and a place to save the money, like a savings account.*

E.   Study the chart.

Modals: *Can* and *Could*			
Subject	Modal	Base	Complement
I, You, He, She, It, We, They	can could	save invest spend	our money my savings his earnings
Use *can* as a modal to express ability or what is possible to do. Use *could* with the same verb to express a suggestion or a possibility.			
We can invest our money in the stock market (expresses ability) We could invest our money in the stock market (expresses ability but only as a suggestion)			

F.   Read each statement and decide if an ability or a possibility is being described. Circle *can* or *could*. Sometimes, both answers are possible, but choose the one that you think fits best.

1. I've seen you do a budget before so I know you _____ do it.   can   could

2. I know you don't have very much in savings, but you _____ open a CD.   can   could

3. She _____ get a second job if she wanted to.   can   could

4. We finally have enough money saved, so now we _____ start a college
   fund for the boys.   can   could

5. You _____ meet with a financial planner if you want to get some advice
   about your finances.   can   could

6. He _____ start buying things online, but he is afraid of his credit card
   number getting stolen.   can   could

7. Jarek just received his checkbook in the mail, so now he _____ start
   writing checks.   can   could

8. Elsie's advisor said she _____ open a 401K since she is self-employed.   can   could

9. The Jacobs family _____ go on vacation because they followed their
   budget and have enough money saved up.   can   could

G. Complete each statement with *can* or *could* and a verb from the box.

increase	invest	give	help	pool	tell	~~look~~	use	afford

1. I _____can look_____ for ways to save more money at home.

2. Jess _____ the computer to do her budget.

3. Derek _____ his money in his friend's restaurant.

4. We _____ our savings to charity.

5. _____ you _____ me reconcile my checking account?

6. _____ you _____ me what bank you use?

7. We _____ our resources and buy the couch together.

8. Brenda _____ her purchasing power by asking for a raise at work.

9. The Salsman family _____ to put a large down payment on a house because of all their liquid assets.

H. Think about your own personal finances and look back at the ideas in Exercise C. Using those ideas or some of your own, write two sets of statements using *can* and *could*.

EXAMPLE: I have been saving money so I can invest in the stock market. I could look for a financial

advisor to give me some ideas on what to invest in.

1. _____

_____

_____

2. _____

_____

_____

LESSON **4** Credit

GOAL ■ Maintain good credit

A. **Complete each suggestion about credit with the correct verb.**

get	use	add	fix	open	establish

1. _____ checking and savings accounts.

2. _____ your credit report.

3. _____ any errors or omissions on your credit report.

4. _____ positive information to your credit report.

5. _____ credit.

6. Once you've got credit, _____ it right.

B. **Discuss the different ways to obtain credit. Number them from *1* to *8*. *1* is the easiest.**

_____ open bank accounts

_____ get and study your credit report

_____ fix your credit report

_____ apply for a bank credit card

_____ apply for a gas credit card

_____ apply for a department store credit card

_____ apply for a major credit card

_____ take out a small loan from your bank

C. Study the chart.

Modals: *Should* and *Ought to* (Advisability)			
Subject	**Modal**	*Have* + **Past Participle**	**Complement**
I, You, He, She, It, We, They	should ought to	have looked	for errors
		have checked	our credit report
Use *should* or *ought to* interchangeably. When used with *have* and the past participle, they express advice about something done in the past.			

D. Change each statement below to the past tense.

1. You should order your credit reports. *You should have ordered your credit reports.*

2. You should check your statement.

   _____

3. He ought to call the bank.

   _____

4. They should find a lower interest rate.

   _____

5. I should start banking online.

   _____

6. We ought to consolidate our credit cards.

   _____

7. I should put money into an IRA.

   _____

E. On a separate piece of paper, change each statement below to the present tense.

1. You should have looked for an account with no fee. *You should look for an account with no fee.*

2. He should have gotten his credit report. _____

3. We shouldn't have ignored the creditors. _____

4. They ought to have canceled their high-interest credit cards. _____

5. I should have contributed more to my 401K. _____

F. Read each situation below and write two statements about what each person should do or should have done.

1. Grayson tried to withdraw money from the ATM, but the machine told her she didn't have any money to withdraw. She knew something was wrong because she had just deposited her paycheck.

   A. _____.

   B. _____.

2. Liam got his credit card statement in the mail and noticed charges for things he didn't buy.

   A. _____.

   B. _____.

3. Christian got a copy of his credit report and noticed that there had been five requests to open credit cards that he didn't initiate. They were from three years ago.

   A. _____.

   B. _____.

4. Mrs. Haverson got a bill in the mail for pay-per-view movies that she didn't order or watch. When she called the cable company, they said they had been ordered from her phone line.

   A. _____.

   B. _____.

G. Look at your choices in Exercise B. Which ones should you do? Write statements.

   EXAMPLE: _I should apply for a department store credit card so I can save 10%._

   1. _____

   2. _____

   3. _____

H. Look back at the ideas in Exercise B. Which ones should you have done in the past? Remember to write statements using *should* or *ought to*.

   EXAMPLE: _I should have fixed my credit report a long time ago._

   1. _____

   2. _____

   3. _____

LESSON **5** Identity theft

GOAL ■ Protect against identity theft

A. **Read the situations below. What might be a possible reason for each problem? List some ideas about what you might be able to do.**

1. A creditor calls you and tells you that you owe them $5,000. You have never dealt with the company before.

   Possible reason: _____

   What you can do: _____

2. Your credit report lists three loans that are not yours.

   Possible reason: _____

   What you can do: _____

3. Your bank account has five dollars in it instead of five hundred dollars.

   Possible reason: _____

   What you can do: _____

4. Your phone bill is double the regular amount this month.

   Possible reason: _____

   What you can do: _____

B. **The following list includes ideas to avoid identity theft. Check (✓) the ones you do.**

☐ Don't purchase things online. _____

☐ Don't purchase things online without a secure connection to the Internet. _____

☐ Check your credit report once a year. _____

☐ Check your credit report once a month. _____

☐ Never give out your social security number except to government agencies and employers. _____

☐ Don't give out personal information like driver's license numbers or bank account numbers to solicitors. _____

☐ Cancel unused credit cards. _____

☐ Shred all bills and statements after five years. _____

☐ Keep your wallet close to you at all times when in public. _____

C. **Prioritize the list of all the items in Exercise B from most important to least important by writing a number after each statement. *1* is the most important.**

D. Study the chart.

Modals: *May, Might,* and *Could* (Uncertainty)			
Subject	**Modal**	*Have* **+ Past Participle**	**Complement**
It		have gotten	stolen online.
Someone, He, She, They	may might could	have found	your social security number.
It		have been	identify theft.
Use modals like *may, might,* and *could* with *have* and the past participle to describe possibility or uncertainty about something that happened in the past. It could have been identity theft. (The speaker doesn't know. He or she is expressing the possibility. He or she is uncertain of what really happened.)			

E. Unscramble the words to write statements of uncertainty.

1. have / could / a bank error / been / it

   It could have been a bank error.

2. your credit card / you / have / might / at the hotel / left

   _____

3. could / he / have / gotten / from an online site / your number

   _____

4. have / your credit report / checked / may / they

   _____

5. seen / they / have / your social security number / might

   _____

6. your / someone / have / seen / pin number / might

   _____

7. she / left / her wallet / could / at the restaurant / have

   _____

F. Complete the statements by choosing a modal (*may, might, could*) and writing the correct form of the verb in parentheses.

1. You _____*might have forgotten*_____ (forget) to shred your credit card statements.

2. She _____ (give) them a fake social security number.

3. They _____ (find) your bank account number.

4. Someone _____ (take) your driver license from your wallet.

5. It _____ (be) identify theft.

G. Use *may, might,* or *could* to write TWO possible explanations for each problem.

EXAMPLE:

Your electricity bill is $100 more than last month.

I might have forgotten to turn the air-conditioning off at night.

We could have left the lights on when we weren't home.

1. You receive a package in the mail with your address but someone else's name on it. You didn't order the package.

   _____

   _____

2. Your checking account has $2,000 more than it should.

   _____

   _____

3. Someone calls your house asking for someone who doesn't live there.

   _____

   _____

4. There is a charge on your credit card bill that you didn't make.

   _____

   _____

PRACTICE TEST

A. Read and circle the correct answers.

A financial counselor helps young couples who are just starting out manage their money and get out of debt. Many couples spend more than they have on their weddings and honeymoons. Some couples have substantial loans and credit card debt. A financial counselor helps people find ways to quickly reduce debt and avoid falling into greater financial hardships. In order to do this, a financial counselor and his or her clients make an agreement.

Our Agreement	
What you will do	**What I will do**
You will make a list of all your assets together as a couple or family.	I will place a value on your assets based on your descriptions.
You will identify all expenditures.	I will help identify ways to save on current expenditures.
You will distinguish between *wants* and *needs*.	I will negotiate with loan agents to reduce debt.
You will prioritize your expenditures.	I will create a payment plan.
You will meet with your financial counselor once a month for the first three months.	I will counsel you at every step of the process. While you are doing each step, I will meet with you to help.
You will follow your financial counselor's advice.	You are accountable for your money. I will give you advice. It is your responsibility to follow the advice.

1. Why do some young couples need financial counseling?
   a. Some have credit card debt.
   b. Some have large loans.
   c. They spend too much money on their wedding and honeymoon.
   d. all of the above

2. According to the agreement, the counselor will . . .
   a. identify all expenditures.
   b. make a list of assets.
   c. create a payment plan.
   d. none of the above

3. According to the agreement, something a couple does not have to do is . . .
   a. distinguish between wants and needs.
   b. negotiate with loan agents to reduce debt.
   c. follow the advice of the counselor.
   d. all of the above

4. Who is responsible for the money?
   a. the couple
   b. both the couple and the counselor
   c. the counselor
   d. neither the couple nor the counselor

UNIT 3
LESSON ① Buying a car

GOAL ■ Purchase a car

A. Look at the information and complete the table.

Year: 2012
Miles: 89,000
Mileage: 12 MPG
Upholstery:
cloth – fair condition
Seats: 8
Additional Information:
GPS
anti-theft device
new tires

Year: 2014
Miles: 45,000
Mileage: 14 MPG
Upholstery:
leather – good condition
Seats: 7
Additional Information:
GPS, Wi-Fi enabled

Year: 2013
Miles: 65,000
Mileage: 12 MPG
Upholstery:
leather – good condition
Seats: 5
Additional Information:
GPS
anti-theft device
premium stereo system

Black SUV		Gray SUV		White SUV	
Pros	Cons	Pros	Cons	Pros	Cons
		low mileage			only seats 5 people

B. What are some questions you might ask about the cars in Exercise A?

1. _____

2. _____

3. _____

4. _____

5. _____

C. Study the chart.

Yes/No and Information Questions	
Yes/No questions	
Past	**Did** the car **perform** well? **Was** it in an accident?
Present	**Does** it **have** airbags? **Is** it still under warranty? **Are** there any tears in the leather?
Future	**Will** it **pass** a smog check?
Present perfect	**Have** you **driven** the car cross-country? **Has** it **had** more than one owner?
Information questions	
Past	Where **did** you **buy** the car? Where **was** the damage?
Present	How often **do** you **change** the oil?
Future	How **will** you come up with a price?
Present perfect	How many owners **has** this car **had**?

D. Fix the mistake in each question below.

        been
1. Has it ~~be~~ in an accident?

2. Have you ever replace the tires?

3. How often do you takes it in for service?

4. When was the last time you taken it in?

5. How many miles do it get to the gallon?

6. Will you allowing me to take it to my mechanic?

7. Where is the license plates?

8. Are it in good condition?

E. Look at the car advertisement. Write questions you might ask about the car using the question types and verb tenses provided.

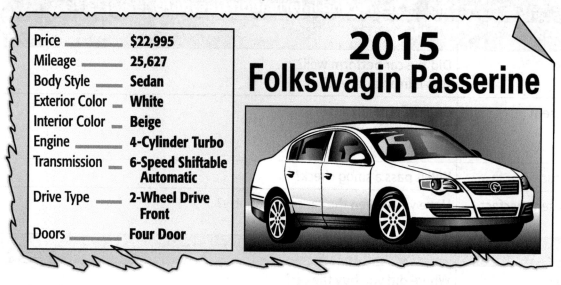

1. (y/n present) _Does it have a beige interior?_ _____

2. (y/n-present perfect) _____

3. (info-future) _____

4. (info-present) _____

5. (info-present perfect) _____

6. (y/n-past) _____

7. (info-past) _____

8. (y/n-future) _____

F. Of the four cars listed in this lesson, which one would you buy? Why?

_____

_____

_____

_____

_____

LESSON **2** Maintenance and repair

GOAL ■ Maintain and repair a car

A. **Complete each phrase below with an appropriate verb. Verbs will be used more than once.**

change	check	replace	inspect	top off

1. _____ your air filter.

2. _____ your oil levels.

3. _____ your wipers.

4. _____ your brakes.

5. _____ your power-steering fluid.

6. _____ and _____ your coolant.

7. _____ and _____ your spark plugs.

8. _____ your washer fluid.

9. _____ your wheel bolts.

B. **Answer the questions. (If you don't own a car, imagine you do.)**

1. Who is your mechanic? _____

2. Where is your mechanic located? _____

3. How often do you rotate your tires? _____

4. When do you change your oil? _____

5. How do you pay for gas? (cash, credit card, etc.) _____

6. Why do you take your car to a mechanic for repairs? _____

7. Whose car do you drive? _____

8. Which gas station do you go to? _____

C. Look back at the questions in Exercise B and underline the question words. Make a list of those words below and decide what type of answer each question word requires.

Question word	Answers
who	name of a person

D. Study the chart.

Question Words and Answers			
	Question word	Question	Sample answer
Location	Where	is the fuel filter?	Next to the dipstick.
Choice	Which	mechanic do you use?	The one on First Street.
Location	Where	do you park your car?	On the street.
People	Who Whose	repairs your car? car is in the garage?	A mechanic. My brother's.
Time	When How often	do you change the oil? do you change the oil?	Every 5,000 miles.
Information	How Why	do you change the oil? do you change the oil?	First, drain the oil. The oil gets dirty.

E. Match each question to an appropriate answer.

1. __f__   Who does your body work?   a. I have the mechanic do it.

2. _____   When do you replace your brakes?   b. About every five years.

3. _____   How do you change your oil?   c. Our garage is full of stuff.

4. _____   Where is your gas tank?   d. My company.

5. _____   How often do you get a new car?   e. My sister's.

6. _____   Why do you park on the street?   f. The Body Shop in Acton.

7. _____   Whose car are you driving?   g. On the driver's side.

8. _____   Who pays for your car insurance?   h. At 50,000 miles.

F. Write a question for each answer below.

1. (My friend.) _Who sold you that car?_ _____

2. (My uncle.) _____

3. (It gets dirty from being parked outside.) _____

4. (Next to the grocery store.) _____

5. (I like SUVs.) _____

6. (Every 3,000 miles.) _____

7. (My brother's.) _____

8. (The one on the corner.) _____

G. Write four questions you could ask about a car. Write the answers you might expect to hear.

1. Q: _____

   A: _____

2. Q: _____

   A: _____

3. Q: _____

   A: _____

4. Q: _____

   A: _____

LESSON **3** **Car insurance**

GOAL ■ Interpret an auto insurance policy

A. Read the conversation.

Amar: Naveen, could you loan me some money? I got into a car accident, and I need to get my car fixed so I can get to work.

Naveen: Don't you have car insurance?

Amar: Yes, but it will take too long to get it fixed if I go through the insurance company.

Naveen: Didn't you call them?

Amar: No, not yet.

Naveen: Well, if you get it fixed on your own, they probably won't reimburse you.

Amar: But isn't that why I pay for the insurance?

Naveen: Yes, but they have to file an accident report and send a representative out to look at the damage. Then, they will get estimates and decide how much they will pay to fix it.

Amar: Why didn't I just take the bus?

B. Write about an experience you've had with an insurance company. What happened? What did the insurance company do?

_____

_____

_____

_____

_____

_____

_____

C. Look at the following pairs of questions. What is the difference in structure and meaning?

1. Don't you have car insurance?   Do you have car insurance?
2. Didn't you call them?   Did you call them?
3. Isn't that why I pay for the insurance?   Is that why I pay for the insurance?
4. Weren't you the one driving the car?   Were you the one driving the car?

D. Study the chart.

Negative Questions				
Auxiliary verb	**Subject**	**Main verb**		**Assumption**
Don't	you	need	insurance?	She **needs** insurance.
Doesn't	she	have	uninsured motorist coverage?	She **has** uninsured motorist coverage.
Didn't	I	help	you fix your car?	I **helped** you fix your car.
Aren't	you		the principal driver?	You are the principal driver.
Isn't	she	driving	30 miles to work every day?	She is **driving** 30 miles to work every day.
Weren't	you	sitting	in the passenger seat?	You were **sitting** in the passenger seat.
We use negative questions when we assume that something is true.				

E. Complete each question with the correct negative form of the verb *do* or *be*. Then, write the assumption below.

1. _____Aren't_____ they both on the insurance policy?

    Assumption: _They are both on the insurance policy._____

2. _____ she get an insurance policy?

    Assumption: _____

3. _____ you the one who bought the car?

    Assumption: _____

4. _____ he call the police officer after the accident?

    Assumption: _____

5. _____ Luisa the one who wanted the high deductible?

    Assumption: _____

F. Change each statement to a negative question.

1. She is covered by her husband's policy.

   Isn't she covered by her husband's policy?

2. The insurance company is paying for the accident.

   _____

3. He has a policy that covers anyone who drives his car.

   _____

4. She called the insurance company five days ago.

   _____

5. They said they would look over the policy and get back to us.

   _____

6. Amar rented a car while his was being fixed.

   _____

G. Read each statement and write an appropriate negative question.

1. She's driving a rental car.

   Doesn't she have a car?

2. They had to pay $3,200 to get their car fixed.

   _____

3. He just added his wife to his auto insurance policy.

   _____

4. We have a $1,500 deductible on our policy.

   _____

5. She doesn't have insurance for her new car yet.

   _____

6. The insurance agent called their house last week.

   _____

LESSON **4** Gas and mileage

GOAL ■ Compute mileage and gas consumption

A. Read Rodolfo's chart and answer the questions.

Trip	Odometer	Trip miles	Gallons	MPG	Cost per gallon	Cost per mile
Start	66,101					
1	66,245	144	4.8	30	$4.75	$.16
2	66,400	155	5.2	29	$4.77	$.16
3	66,710	310	11	27	$4.73	$.17
	AVERAGE	200	7	28.6	$4.75	$.16

Look at Trip 1:

1. How many miles to the gallon did Rodolfo get? _____

2. How many gallons did he use? _____

3. What was his odometer reading at the end of the trip? _____

4. How much did he spend per gallon? _____

Look at Trip 2:

1. What was his odometer reading at the beginning of the trip? _____

2. What was his cost per mile? _____

3. What was his average MPG? _____

4. How many miles did Rodolfo drive? _____

Look at Trip 3:

1. How many miles did Rodolfo drive? _____

2. How many gallons did he use? _____

3. How much did he spend per gallon? _____

4. What was his odometer reading at the end of the trip? _____

B. Fill in the table using the information for all three trips in Exercise A.

Questions	Answers
How many miles did Rodolfo drive?	609 miles
How much gas did he use?	
How much did he spend?	
What was the starting odometer reading?	
What were the average trip miles?	
What was the average cost per mile?	
What was the average MPG?	
What was the ending odometer reading?	

C. Imagine that a friend is asking you questions about a driving trip. Match the questions to the correct answers.

1. _____   How much gas did you put in?   a. 45,987.

2. _____   What was the cost per gallon?   b. 19 cents.

3. _____   What was the odometer reading?   c. $4.33.

4. __h__   How many miles did you drive?   d. 355 miles.

5. _____   What were the average trip miles?   e. $46.87.

6. _____   What was the cost per mile?   f. 12 gallons.

7. _____   How much did you spend?   g. 24 MPG.

8. _____   What is your average MPG?   ~~h.~~ 254 miles.

D. Write a question that goes with each answer given.

1. (255 miles.) How many miles did you drive? _____

2. (15 cents.) _____

3. ($52.76.) _____

4. (110,465.) _____

E. Unscramble the words to write questions. Then, choose an appropriate answer from the box.

~~16 gallons~~	About $60.	About 19.
15 cents.	About 35,000 miles.	About 230.

1. much / gas / do / put / you / week / in / each / how

   Q: _How much gas do you put in each week?_   A: _16 gallons._

2. miles / do / per / you / many / week / drive / how

   Q: _____   A: _____

3. odometer / right / what / your / is / now / reading

   Q: _____   A: _____

4. is / what / MPG / your

   Q: _____   A: _____

5. is / mile / cost / what / average / per / your

   Q: _____   A: _____

6. much / gas / do / on / spend / week / per / how / you

   Q: _____   A: _____

F. Fill in the missing numbers in the table below.

Date	Odometer	Trip miles	Gallons	MPG	Cost per gallon	Cost per mile
1/15	47,879	256	12		$4.10	
1/26		310	14		$3.95	
2/11		300	14		$4.05	
2/23		278	13		$3.98	
	AVERAGE					

LESSON ⑤ Traffic laws

GOAL ■ Follow the rules of the road

A. Read each of the statements below and decide if they are _true_ or _false_.

1. _____true_____ Teenagers have higher insurance rates than adults.

2. _____ Men are better drivers than women.

3. _____ Elderly people cause more accidents than middle-aged people.

4. _____ Bigger people can handle their alcohol better so they can drink and still drive.

5. _____ You should always warm up your car before you begin driving.

6. _____ You will be safe from a tornado if you stay in your car.

B. Answer the questions below based on your answers the statements in Exercise A.

1. Who has higher insurance rates than adults? _____teenagers_____

2. Who drives better than women? _____

3. Who causes more accidents than middle-aged people? _____

4. What can bigger people do? _____

5. What should you do before driving your car? _____

6. What will you be safe from if you stay in your car? _____

C. Look at the example below and complete each question with the correct words.

EXAMPLE: Teenagers have higher insurance rates, <u>don't they</u>?

1. Men are better drivers than women, _____?

2. Elderly people cause more accidents than middle-aged people, _____?

3. Bigger people can handle their alcohol better, _____?

4. You should always warm up your car before you begin driving, _____?

5. You will be safe from a tornado if you stay in your car, _____?

D. Study the charts.

Tag Questions		
	Negative statement + affirmative tag	**Affirmative statement + negative tag**
Past	He didn't sell his car, did he?	He sold his car, didn't he?
Past Perfect	You hadn't bought a car, had you?	You had bought a car, hadn't you?
Past Progressive	He wasn't driving, was he?	He was driving, wasn't he?
Present	She isn't the driver, is she?	She's the driver, isn't she?
Present Progressive	I wasn't driving the speed limit, was I?	I was driving the speed limit, wasn't I?
Present Perfect	He hasn't been drinking, has he?	He's been drinking, hasn't he?
Future	She won't take her car to work, will she?	She'll take her car to work, won't she?
• Tag questions are used to check if something is true or to ask for agreement. • A tag question uses an auxiliary verb + a subject pronoun. • The tag question uses the same tense as the main verb. • Negative tags are usually contracted.		

	Affirmative tag (nobody, no one, nothing)	**Affirmative statement + negative tag**
Past	Nobody wants an accident, do they?	Everybody knew the risks, didn't they?
Present	Nothing is more important, is it?	Everyone buys insurance, don't they?
Future	No one will buy it, will they?	Somebody will come, won't they?
	Use *they* with *nobody, no one, someone, somebody, everyone,* and *everybody.* Use *it* with *nothing.*	

E. Circle the correct tag question for each statement.

1. He'll look for a new car, <u>doesn't he</u> / (<u>won't he</u>)?

2. She isn't carpooling anymore, <u>is she</u> / <u>isn't she</u>?

3. Nobody walks to school, <u>will they</u> / <u>do they</u>?

4. Gas has gotten expensive, <u>has it</u> / <u>hasn't it</u>?

5. I don't have time to pick you up, <u>don't I</u> / <u>do I</u>?

6. Hybrid cars have gone up in price, <u>have they</u> / <u>haven't they</u>?

F. Complete each statement with the correct tag.

1. We have to have insurance, ___don't we___?

2. She didn't lease a new car, _____?

3. They traded in their car, _____?

4. You saw the police officer, _____?

5. We won't be able to carpool in the morning, _____?

6. You aren't parking in my parking space, _____?

7. You hadn't been to the store, _____?

8. You have to stop for pedestrians in a crosswalk, _____?

9. I have to pay for the accident, _____?

10. She wasn't drinking, _____?

G. Think of some rules related to driving that you are unsure of. Write six tag questions you could ask a police officer.

EXAMPLE: _My 8-year-old daughter can sit in front seat, can't she?_

1. _____, _____

2. _____, _____

3. _____, _____

4. _____, _____

5. _____, _____

6. _____, _____

PRACTICE TEST

A. Read and circle the best answers.

Year: 2014
MPG: 22 City, 32 Hwy
Price: $25,000
4-door sedan
white
Automatic Transmission
Cloth Upholstery

Year: 2012
MPG: 18 City, 25 Hwy
Price: $42,895
SUV
blue
Automatic Transmission
Cloth Upholstery

Year: 2015
MPG: 30 City, 36 Hwy
Price: $28,687
truck
green
Manual Transmission
Leather Upholstery

1. Which car is the most expensive?

    a. the 4-door sedan

    b. the truck

    c. the SUV

    d. none of the above

2. Which car gets the best miles per gallon?

    a. the 4-door sedan

    b. the truck

    c. the SUV

    d. They all the get the same miles per gallon.

3. What makes the truck different from the other two?

    a. the color

    b. the price

    c. the material the seats are made of

    d. all of the above

4. Which car is the oldest?

    a. the 4-door sedan

    b. the truck

    c. the SUV

    d. They are all the same age.

LESSON **1** I have a problem

GOAL ■ Communicate issues by phone

A. Landlords usually inspect recently vacated properties. Look at the list below and decide who a landlord would call from the box.

painter	plumber	handyman	electrician
pest control	locksmith	cleaner	

☐ paint is peeling *painter* _____

☐ holes in walls _____

☐ pipe leaks _____

☐ ceiling leaks _____

☐ electrical outlets don't work _____

☐ dirty countertops _____

☐ dirty floors and walls _____

☐ dirty carpets _____

☐ insect infestation _____

☐ doors don't close properly _____

☐ locks on windows not functioning _____

☐ locks on doors not functioning _____

B. Look at the conversation below. Write two more conversations using the information from Exercise A.

A: Who will fix *the peeling paint*?

B: The landlord will get *a painter* to come.

1. **A:** _____

   B: _____

2. **A:** _____

   B: _____

C. Study the chart.

Causative Verbs: *Get, Have, Help, Make, Let*			
Subject	**Verb**	**Noun/Pronoun (object)**	**Infinitive (omit *to* except with *get*)**
He	will get	his handyman	to come.
She	had	her mom	wait for the repairman.
The landlord	helped	me	move in.
Melanie	makes	her sister	pay half of the rent.
Mr. Martin	let	Melanie	skip one month's rent.
Transitive verbs are verbs that require a direct object. Causative verbs are usually transitive verbs.			

D. Unscramble the words to write causative statements.

1. them / had / the handyman / under the mat / leave a key

   The handyman had them leave a key under the mat.

2. the tenants / him / let / out front / put / a *For Sale* sign

   _____

3. made / my landlord / the holes in the wall / patch / me /

   _____

4. the landlord / for a month / us / will get / I / to give / free rent

   _____

5. her boyfriend / she / which couch to buy / decide / let

   _____

6. pay / my aunt / me / rent / helped / for a few months

   _____

E.   Choose a word or phrase from each column to write causative statements.

A	B	C	D
her parents	got	~~her friends~~	move in
his cousin	~~had~~	his tenants	pay an extra security deposit for the dog
I	have	my mom	pay half the utilities
~~she~~	made	their friends	~~repair the damage they caused~~
the landlord	were helping	their neighbors	sleep on the couch for a few days
the renters	will let	us	to pay for the party

1. She had her friends repair the damage they caused.

2. _____

3. _____

4. _____

5. _____

6. _____

F.   Imagine you are the landlord of a three-bedroom house. Read each problem below and write a causative statement to say what you would do. Try to use a different verb for each statement.

Problem: There is a broken window in one of the bedrooms.

Solution: I will get my handyman to repair the window.

Problem: The sprinkler head is broken and spraying water everywhere.

Solution: _____

Problem: There is a cockroach infestation in the kitchen.

Solution: _____

Problem: The roof is leaking after the most recent storm.

Solution: _____

LESSON ② Understand the fine print

GOAL ■ Interpret rental agreements

A. Look at the problems in an apartment for rent and put them into the correct categories. Are they problems you *hear, see,* or *smell*?

Problems
dirt
insects
rodents in walls
strange odor from carpet
neighbors playing loud music
noisy pipes
holes in walls
uncollected garbage

See

dirt
_____
_____
_____
_____

Hear

_____
_____
_____
_____
_____

Smell

_____
_____
_____
_____

B. Add two more problems to each list in Exercise A.

C. Study the chart.

Perceptive Verbs		
Subject + verb	**Direct object**	**Gerund or base**
Simple Present		
I see/watch/look at	the landlord	fixing the sink.
I notice/observe	the gardener	clipping bushes on Tuesdays.
I feel	the light switch in the dark.	
I hear/listen to	music	filling the room.
I smell	a strange odor.	
Simple Past		
I saw/watched/looked at	my neighbor	water (watering) the plants.
I noticed/observed	everything that went on there.	
I felt	the cold water	run (running).
I heard/listened to	noises	come (coming) from upstairs.
I smelled	a sweet smell.	
Transitive verbs require a direct object. Perception verbs are usually transitive verbs.		
In the present tense, use the gerund if needed after the direct object. Note: In most of the examples above, the gerund is not needed. It just adds more information.		
In the past tense, use the base or gerund after the direct object.		

D. Complete each sentence with a direct object. Add a gerund or base verb if you need to make your sentences clearer.

1. My neighbor smelled *the fire* _____.

2. Her uncle was watching _____.

3. She had been listening to _____.

4. Her brother had noticed _____.

5. We are looking at _____.

6. I observed _____.

7. She feels _____.

8. The realtor heard _____.

E. **Choose a perception verb and complete each sentence below. Use the verb tense indicated.**

1. (present progressive) His mother _is listening to_ the emergency broadcast on the radio.

2. (future perfect progressive) We _____ the construction for three years by the time it is finished.

3. (past) I _____ the air-conditioning turn off.

4. (future) The landlord _____ at the entire apartment to see if it was cleaned properly.

5. (present perfect progressive) He _____ at that same house for sale for almost a year.

6. (present) I _____ music coming from the condo next door.

7. (past perfect) She _____ the gas before she called the gas company.

8. (past) Her husband _____ the unlocked door.

9. (present perfect) We _____ so many young tenants move into this building.

10. (future perfect) Her nephews _____ by the time we get there.

F. **Imagine you are a landlord writing a rental agreement. What do you think your responsibility should be for each of the items listed below?**

1. Pest control: _I should make sure that there are no pests in the rental._____

2. Phone service: _____

3. Smoke detectors: _____

4. Electricity: _____

5. Satellite/Cable TV: _____

6. Maintenance of yard: _____

LESSON ③ Your rights

GOAL ■ Identify tenant and landlord rights

A. Read the e-mail that Jonathan wrote to his landlord.

⊗ ⊖ ⊕

📩 Send Now   📨 Send Later   📥 Save as Draft   🗑 Delete   📎 Add Attachment   ✒ Signature

To:
Cc:
Subject:

Dear Mr. Michelson,

My name is Jonathan Appleby. My wife and I rent the apartment at 3765 West Birch Street. We have been at this residence for three years and faithfully pay the rent on time and keep our end of the rental agreement. I am writing this e-mail to document all of the problems that we are now facing in our apartment. This is our second e-mail to you. Please look over these issues as soon as possible.

First, the plumbing is becoming more of a problem every day. The leaking is getting worse. The plumbing is one of the issues that I mentioned in my previous letter. We wake up every morning with water on the bathroom floor coming from the sink. It is dangerous. My wife slipped yesterday. Fortunately, she was not injured, but I hope you will see that this problem is corrected within the next few days.

I also remind you of the time when we saw termites in the house. This is no longer a problem inside and the common areas are not our responsibility, but I have seen flying insects outside and I suspect they are termites. You may want to resolve this potential problem soon as well.

Finally, the handyman who came last week said that our carpet should be replaced. Have you heard from him? He sounded very definite about it. It would be a great improvement if this could also be taken care of.

Thank you for your attention,

Jonathan Appleby

B. What are the problems Jonathan mentions in his e-mail?

1. _____

_____

2. _____

_____

3. _____

_____

C. Study the chart.

Types	Example sentence	Refers to
Things	The plumbing is one of the issues *that* I mentioned in my previous letter.	*that* refers to *plumbing*
Time	I remind you of the time *when* we saw termites in the house.	*when* refers to *the time*
People	The handyman *who* came last week…	*who* refers to *the handyman*
Place	That is a place *where* I would never live	*where* refers to *a place*
The phrases that begin with a relative pronoun are called restrictive adjective clauses. Restrictive adjective clauses give essential information about the noun they refer to. They cannot be omitted without losing the meaning of the sentence.		

D. Write the correct relative pronoun in each sentence below.

1. Did you ever find the lease agreement _____*that*_____ I left on the counter?

2. He will never forget the time _____ he didn't get his security deposit back.

3. I want to look for a place in the city _____ you live.

4. Renting an apartment is one thing _____ I hope I will never have to do again.

5. She is the woman _____ found this apartment for us.

6. That is the apartment _____ they found the million dollars.

7. The painter _____ finished our house is a good friend of mine.

8. This is a house _____ we could live for the rest of our lives.

E. Match each statement with the appropriate adjective clause.

1. _____ She's renting the condo   a. who didn't return my security deposit.

2. _____ That's the landlord   b. where I can have my two dogs.

3. _____ Can we find a time   c. where her parents used to live.

4. _____ They are the friends   d. that I will never understand.

5. _____ I want to find a place   e. who helped me move into my new place.

6. _____ That is one thing   f. when we can go over the lease together?

F. Find the errors in each sentence below.

1. I'm ~~wiritng~~ *writing* this letter on behalf of all of the ~~resident~~ *residents*, who live at Crystal ~~cove~~ *Cove*.

2. Sometimes at night, the guard isn't not in the booth where he is suppose to be.

3. At times, I have see him let people in who don't lived here and aren't visit anyone who live here.

4. A friend who visited me said he give them the gate code so they could get in any time they wanted.

5. In adition to all of these problems, he is not very freindly to the residents who live here.

6. These are issues that need a response, so please let us know what you plans to do.

G. Rewrite the sentences above in paragraph format.

_____

_____

_____

_____

_____

H. Write an e-mail message to a landlord to complain about three different problems in your apartment. Remember to use relative pronouns.

_____

_____

_____

_____

_____

_____

_____

_____

_____

LESSON **4** Insuring your home

GOAL ■ Get insurance

A. Compare the two insurance quotes and circle the best answers.

Renter's Insurance QUOTE #1		Renter's Insurance QUOTE #2	
Value of Personal Property	$29,000	Value of Personal Property	$35,000
Deductible	$250	Deductible	$500
Liability	$100,000	Liability	$75,000
Medical Payments	$1,000	Medical Payments	$2,000
Annual Premium	$220.07	Annual Premium	$265.80
Monthly Payment	$18.34	Monthly Payment	$22.15

1. Which quote pays the least for medical payments?   #1   #2

2. Which quote has a higher deductible?   #1   #2

3. Which quote costs more each month?   #1   #2

4. Which quote is better for you?   #1   #2

B. Write an explanation why one of the quotes in Exercise A is better for you than the other.

_____

_____

_____

_____

_____

C. Study the charts.

Comparative and Superlative Adjectives			
Type of adjective	**Simple form**	**Comparative form**	**Superlative form**
One-syllable adjectives	high	**higher**	**the highest**
One-syllable adjectives that end in -**e**	nice	**nicer**	**the nicest**
One-syllable adjectives that end in *consonant-vowel-consonant*	big	**bigger**	**the biggest**
Two-syllable adjectives that end in -**y**	messy	**messier**	**the messiest**
Other two-syllable adjectives	decent	**more decent**	**the most decent**
Some two-syllable adjectives have two forms.	quiet friendly	**quieter** or **more quiet** **friendlier** or **more friendly**	**the quietest** or **the most quiet** **the friendliest** or **the most friendly**
Adjectives with three or more syllables	expensive	**more expensive**	**the most expensive**

- Use the comparative form to compare two things.
- If the second item is expressed, use **than**.
  My apartment is **bigger than** hers.
- Use the superlative form to compare one thing to two or more things.
- A prepositional phrase is sometimes used at the end of a superlative sentence.
  My insurance agent is the nicest **in the business**.

	Simple form	Comparative form	Superlative form
Irregular Adjectives	good bad far little much/many	better worse farther less more	the best the worst the farthest the least the most
Irregular Adverbs	well badly a little a lot	better worse less more	the best the worst the least the most

D. **Write comparative or superlative sentences. Use *than* when comparing two things.**

1. his deductible is / high _____ His deductible is the highest. _____

2. this estimate is / cheap / the first one we got _____

3. that company has / reputable service / our current one _____

4. her rate is / low / mine _____

5. your quote is / expensive _____

6. my insurance company has / good / online service _____

E. **Write comparative or superlative sentences using the words in parentheses.**

1. I have an apartment. (spacious / in my building)

   I have the most spacious apartment in my building. _____

2. Before getting renter's insurance, you should compare quotes. (low / you can find)

   _____

3. She is using an insurance agency that charges a fee. (high / of all the agencies)

   _____

4. I plan to negotiate with the agent. (motivated / other agents)

   _____

5. We found an insurance company. (decent / in the business)

   _____

F. **Using the quotes in Exercise A as a guide, come up with your own insurance quote.**

Renter's Insurance QUOTE			
Value of Personal Property	_____	Medical Payments	_____
Deductible	_____	Annual Premium	_____
Liability	_____	Monthly Payment	_____

LESSON **5** **Protecting your home**

GOAL ■ Prevent theft

A. **What is the difference between a burglar and a thief?**

Burglar: _____

Thief: _____

B. **Write a sentence with each of the words below.**

1. theft: _____

2. burglary: _____

3. thief: _____

4. burglarize: _____

C. **Check (✓) the items that could help prevent a burglar from entering your home.**

☐ Get a cat.

☐ Leave the television on when you're not home.

☐ Plant trees in front of your home.

☐ Lock up your valuables.

☐ Organize a neighborhood watch.

☐ Keep your artwork near the windows.

☐ Put locks on your patio doors.

☐ Install an alarm system.

☐ Board your dog when you go away.

☐ _____

☐ _____

☐ _____

D. **Add three more ideas to the list in Exercise C.**

E. Study the chart.

Example sentence	Passive subject	Be	Past participle	by + person (optional)
The house was built in 1974.	the house	was	built	
The home will be monitored by the alarm company.	the home	will be	monitored	by the alarm company
The bills are paid by the insurance company.	the bills	are	paid	by the insurance company
It is estimated that a home is broken into every minute.	it	is	estimated	

Use the passive voice to emphasize the object of the action, or when the doer of the action is unknown or unimportant.

To change an active sentence to a passive, switch the subject and the object and change the verb to the correct tense of *be* + the past participle. The word *by* is used before the doer of the action.

F. Circle the correct passive voice form.

1. The new homes be built / (are built) with energy-efficient heating and cooling.

2. The man with the gun was found / was find at the local market.

3. The terms of the lease can be found / can be find on the landlord's website.

4. The condo was sell / was sold for a reasonable price.

5. Their new home was broke into / was broken into last night.

6. Her water heater will be repaired / will repaired by a handyman.

7. His bills are being paid / are be paid by the insurance company.

8. Homes for sale can be lease / can be leased until the owner finds a buyer.

G. **Change each active sentence to a passive one. Keep the verb tenses the same.**

1. We will add renter's insurance to our policy.

   Renter's insurance will be added to our policy.

2. The thieves took all of our tools from the garage.

   _____

3. The appraiser appraised our home last week.

   _____

4. The loan officer funded our loan before escrow closed.

   _____

5. The handyman will repair the damage from the fire.

   _____

6. He thinks a local gang stole his truck from in front of his house.

   _____

H. **Imagine you are forming a neighborhood watch group. Write statements in the passive voice form about what your group will do to prevent theft.**

1. _____

2. _____

3. _____

4. _____

5. _____

6. _____

PRACTICE TEST

A. Read the e-mail and circle the best answers.

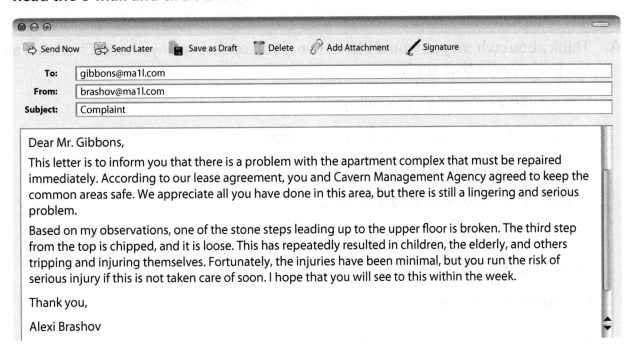

Dear Mr. Gibbons,

This letter is to inform you that there is a problem with the apartment complex that must be repaired immediately. According to our lease agreement, you and Cavern Management Agency agreed to keep the common areas safe. We appreciate all you have done in this area, but there is still a lingering and serious problem.

Based on my observations, one of the stone steps leading up to the upper floor is broken. The third step from the top is chipped, and it is loose. This has repeatedly resulted in children, the elderly, and others tripping and injuring themselves. Fortunately, the injuries have been minimal, but you run the risk of serious injury if this is not taken care of soon. I hope that you will see to this within the week.

Thank you,

Alexi Brashov

1. Who is the landlord?
   a. Alexi Brashov
   b. Mr. Gibbons
   c. Alexi and Mr. Gibbons
   d. neither Alexi nor Mr. Gibbons

2. What is the problem?
   a. Children have tripped on a broken step.
   b. One of the steps is chipped.
   c. The elderly have injured themselves.
   d. all of the above

3. When would the tenant like the problem fixed?
   a. immediately
   b. by next month
   c. next year
   d. within the week

4. What is the purpose of the e-mail?
   a. to ask the landlord to pay for the hospital bills of the elderly that have fallen
   b. to let the landlord know that there is a problem
   c. to find out how much it will cost to repair the steps
   d. to get the management agency in trouble for not doing their job

GOAL ■ Identify practices that promote mental and physical well-being

A. **Think about where you would like to live if you could live anywhere. Check (✓) all the preferences that apply.**

☐ I want to live where I can go running every day.

☐ I want to live wherever the mountains are nearby.

☐ I want to live anywhere I can see the ocean.

☐ I want to live anywhere there is no pollution.

☐ I want to live somewhere the sun shines.

☐ I want to live where I can grow my own food.

☐ I want to live wherever my friends live.

☐ I want to live where it is not too hot.

☐ _____

☐ _____

☐ _____

☐ _____

B. **Add your own preferences to the list in Exercise A.**

C. **Based on your preferences, list some of the cities where you would like to live?**

1. _____

2. _____

3. _____

4. _____

D. Look back at Exercise A. Underline each clause that starts with *where*, *wherever*, *somewhere*, or *anywhere*.

EXAMPLE: I want to live <u>where I can go running every day.</u>

E. Study the chart.

Adverbial Clauses of Place		
Main clause	**Subordinate conjunction**	**Subordinate clause (dependent clause)**
I want to live	where, somewhere	I can go running in the morning.
I try to exercise	wherever	I can find a place.
He found a gym	everywhere	he went.
He didn't find a gym	anywhere	he went.
Many times, the place clause can go first and is offset from the main clause by a comma.		
Wherever I find a place, I exercise. Everywhere he went, he found a gym.	Where he was, he was happy. Anywhere he lived, he was unsatisfied.	
Subordinate adverbial clauses have a subject and verb construction, but are dependent on the main clause for their meaning.		

F. Underline the subordinate adverbial clause.

1. I want to live <u>where I can exercise outside every day.</u>

2. Anywhere they can see the ocean, they want to live.

3. I want to live anywhere there is no pollution.

4. Wherever the sun shines, Kimla wants to live.

5. I want to live somewhere I can grow my own food.

6. Wherever my friends live, I want to live.

G. Unscramble the words to write adverbial clauses.

1. the / wherever / is / air / clean

   wherever the air is clean

2. the / wherever / is / and / organic / food / fresh

   _____

3. a cool breeze / I / on / feel / where / my face / can

   _____

4. safe / anywhere / is / thinks / she

   _____

5. there / wherever / is / light / a lot / of

   _____

6. are / anywhere / the / offices / sanitary

   _____

H. Using the adverbial clauses you wrote in Exercise G, write complete sentences.

1. *I like to play soccer wherever the air is clean.*_____

2. _____

3. _____

4. _____

5. _____

6. _____

I. Look back at the information in exercises A and C and write a paragraph about your ideal place to live. Remember to use adverbial clauses of place.

_____

_____

_____

_____

LESSON ② What's this charge for?

GOAL ■ Ask about medical bills

A. Read the conversation.

Receptionist: Dr. Franklin's office.

Patient: Hi. My name is Orlando Colato. I have some questions about my bill.

Receptionist: Of course, Mr. Colato. Let me pull your file. Um, we have two Orlando Colatos. What's your date of birth?

Patient: It's August 12, 1962.

Receptionist: OK, I have it right here. This shows that you owe over $2,000.

Patient: Yes, I know, but the bill is incorrect.

Receptionist: What seems to be wrong?

Patient: This bill shows that I had three examinations in March. First, it says I had a physical for $280 and then a second physical with an X-ray for $398. Finally, it shows another procedure I'm not even familiar with.

Receptionist: Our records show you came in for each appointment, sir.

Patient: I did come in for a physical, but I didn't have an X-ray. After I came in for that appointment, I didn't come in again in March.

Receptionist: You know, I think we confused you with the other patient with your same name.

Patient: Yes, that makes sense. Can you please correct it?

Receptionist: Yes, of course. I'll call you after I've entered the changes.

Patient: OK, as soon as you clear this up, I'll be happy to pay my bill.

Receptionist: OK, thanks for calling and sorry for the inconvenience.

B. Imagine you are the receptionist in Exercise A. Write a summary of the error. Make sure you write the events in chronological order.

_____

_____

_____

_____

_____

C. Study the chart.

Adverbial Clauses of Time		
Main clause (independent clause)	Subordinate conjunction	Subordinate clause (dependent clause)
I spoke to you	after	you examined me on Friday.
Don't pay anything	before	you get an itemized bill.
She felt worse	when	she saw the bill.
He paid the co-pay	while	she was being examined.
We'll send you a bill	as soon as	your insurance pays their portion.
She explained the situation	once	the patient calmed down.
The time clause can also go first and is followed by a comma.		
When you called me on Friday, I spoke to you. While she was being examined, he paid the co-pay.		
Subordinate adverbial clauses have a subject and verb construction, but they are dependent on the main clause for their meaning.		

D. Circle the adverbial time clause in each statement below.

1. (When the nurse called her name,) Kate went in for her appointment.

2. He filled his prescription as soon as he left the doctor's office.

3. While her sister was waiting in the car, she quickly ran in to fill out the form.

4. I called the insurance company after I got the hospital bill.

5. The doctor finished the exam before his next patient arrived.

6. Once the insurance company fixed the mistake, we felt much better.

7. When the insurance representative called, we were out to lunch.

E. Complete each phrase below with a subordinate clause.

1. I called the insurance company after _____.

2. The doctor explained the benefits while _____.

3. They left the office as soon as _____.

F. **Join each main clause and subordinate clause with a subordinating conjunction.**

1. I called the office. They sent me an itemized bill.

   After I called the office, they sent me an itemized bill. _____

2. She got a call from the insurance company. She filled out the application.

   _____

3. The nurse explained the charges. He discussed the charges with his wife.

   _____

4. Liza called the doctor's office. They sent her a duplicate bill.

   _____

5. She recovered from surgery. She went back to work.

   _____

6. She called her family and friends. Dinuka received her diagnosis.

   _____

7. Brent got laid off from work. He starting looking for private insurance.

   _____

G. **Think about a recent experience you have had with a doctor, hospital, or insurance company. Write a brief summary of your experience using sentences with adverbial time clauses. Make some notes below about the order of events and then write your summary.**

1. _____   2. _____

3. _____   4. _____

5. _____   6. _____

7. _____   8. _____

_____

_____

_____

_____

_____

_____

LESSON ③ Health insurance

GOAL ■ Interpret health insurance information

A. Look at the information about PPOs and HMOs.

PPO	HMO
Higher co-pay	Low or sometimes free co-pay
Higher out-of-pocket expenses	Low or sometimes no out-of-pocket expenses
You can see any doctor you want to at any time.	You must choose one primary care physician. You must get a referral from your primary care physician to see another doctor.
Higher monthly premium	Lower monthly premium

B. What do these vocabulary expressions mean? Write definitions.

1. co-pay: _____

2. out-of-pocket: _____

3. monthly premium: _____

4. primary care physician: _____

5. referral: _____

C. What are the advantages of PPOs and HMOs? Make a list.

PPO Advantages

_____

_____

_____

HMO Advantages

_____

_____

_____

D. What are the disadvantages of PPOs and HMOs? Make a list.

PPO Disadvantages

_____

_____

_____

HMO Disadvantages

_____

_____

_____

E. Do you prefer PPO or HMO? Explain why on a separate piece of paper.

F. Study the chart.

Adverbial Clauses of Reason		
Main clause	**Subordinate conjunction**	**Subordinate clause (dependent clause)**
Health insurance is important	because	you never know when there might be an emergency.
The insurance paid the bill	since	we paid all the premiums on time.
The insurance questioned the charges	as	we had quite a few visits in one month.
You can get hip surgery	now that	you have health insurance.
He will keep the PPO	as long as	the premiums don't get too expensive.
The reason clause can also go first and is followed by a comma.		
Since we paid all the premiums on time, the insurance paid the bill. As long as the premiums don't get too expensive, he will keep the PPO.		
Subordinate adverbial clauses have a subject and verb construction, but they are dependent on the main clause for their meaning. Adverbial clauses of reason tell why something happens or is done.		

G. Match each main clause to a subordinate clause to make complete sentences.

1. __e__ He can see any doctor he wants

2. _____ Owen and his brother need insurance

3. _____ They had to mail in their co-pay

4. _____ As long as she stays healthy

5. _____ My company will stay with the same insurance

6. _____ He thinks he doesn't need insurance

7. _____ It's hard to get insurance

8. _____ Now that all the surgeries are over

9. _____ Since she has a pre-existing condition

10. _____ Her bills were outrageous

a. since they forgot to pay it at the office.

b. as long as the employees are happy with it.

c. as he never gets sick.

d. since you smoke.

e. because he has a PPO.

f. she can't find insurance coverage.

g. since she doesn't have insurance.

h. she will begin physical therapy.

i. now that they have started a new business.

j. her premiums will be low.

H. Complete each main clause with an adverbial clause of reason.

1. He will never use that company again because _their fees were too high_ .

2. Her bills are all paid now that _____ .

3. He started exercising five days a week because _____ .

4. The doctor said she could eat red meat again as long as _____ .

5. Since _____ , the insurance company denied the claim.

I. Complete each adverbial clause of reason with a main clause.

1. _He had to call the insurance company five times_ _____ since they weren't returning his calls.

2. As long as you pay your co-pays, _____ .

3. _____ because he never eats fruit and vegetables.

4. _____ as they never paid the bill.

5. Now that she is well again, _____ .

J. Answer each question about yourself using adverbial clauses of reason.

1. Do you eat healthy food every day?

    _____

2. Do you exercise?

    _____

3. Do you go to the doctor for regular check-ups?

    _____

K. Think about what insurance plan would be best for the following people/families. Write *HMO* or *PPO* on the lines and write sentences using adverbial clauses of reason.

1. A family of six where the mother is a teacher and the father stays at home with the kids

    _____

2. A single lawyer who rarely goes to the doctor

    _____

3. A man who has a variety of different health problems and likes to find his own specialists

    _____

LESSON 4 Addictions

GOAL ■ Identify addictions

A. Write a sign of each addiction below.

1. caffeine: *A person has to have a cup of coffee every morning or he or she gets a headache.*

2. gambling: _____

3. shopping: _____

4. Internet: _____

5. TV: _____

6. nicotine: _____

B. Match each word to its synonym by drawing a line.

addict	purification
dependence	removal
detoxification	fanatic
impairment	deterioration
tolerance	obsession
withdrawal	endurance

C. What are some other words related to the word *addiction*?

_____

_____

_____

_____

D. Study the chart.

Adverbial Clauses of Concession		
Main clause	**Subordinate conjunction**	**Subordinate clause (dependent clause)**
He says he doesn't have a gambling problem	although	he spends a lot of time in Vegas.
She tries to stop eating so much	though	she still eats over 4,000 calories a day.
He smokes three packs of cigarettes a day	even though	he says he is quitting.
We are good students	in spite of the fact that	we are addicted to shopping.
The doctor said to take the medicine	even if	I don't like the taste.
* *though* is the same as *although*, but less formal. *Even though* shows a stronger contrast.		
The clause of concession can always go first and is offset from the main clause by a comma.		
Although he spends a lot of time in Vegas, he says he doesn't have a gambling problem. Even though he says he is quitting, he smokes three packs of cigarettes a day.		
Subordinate adverbial clauses have a subject and verb construction, but they are dependent on the main clause for their meaning. Adverbial clauses of concession show a contrast to the main clause.		

E. Circle the subordinate conjunction and underline the subordinate clause.

1. She rides her bike every day (in spite of the fact) it rains three days a week.

2. The doctor asked her to stop drinking even though she only has one glass per week.

3. He doesn't like to run although he does it three times a week.

4. I take my vitamins every day in spite of the fact that I don't like swallowing pills.

5. They take a walk after dinner every night even if they don't feel like it.

F. Choose one main clause and one subordinate clause and write complete sentences.

Main	Subordinate
he says he is not obsessive-compulsive she spends her days in front of the computer surfing the web ~~she insists she does not have a sweet tooth~~ he goes to the mall at least once a day he exercises up to three times a day	though she says she is not addicted to the Internet even though he thinks he doesn't have a problem although he says he is not a shopaholic ~~in spite of the fact that she eats a piece of chocolate after every meal~~ though he washes his hands at least 20 times a day

EXAMPLE: <u>She insists she does not have a sweet tooth in spite of the fact that she eats</u>

<u>a piece of chocolate after every meal.</u>

1. _____

_____

2. _____

_____

3. _____

_____

4. _____

_____

G. Look back at the ideas you wrote for Exercise A. Make statements using the conjunction in parentheses.

1. (even though) <u>Even though she has to have a cup of coffee every morning or she gets a</u>

<u>headache, she says she is not addicted to caffeine.</u>

2. (although) _____

_____

3. (in spite of the fact that) _____

_____

4. (though)_____

_____

5. (even though)_____

_____

6. (in spite of the fact that) _____

_____

LESSON **5** First aid

GOAL ■ Interpret procedures for first aid

A. Match the questions with the correct answers.

Questions:

_____ 1. Why call a poison control center?

_____ 2. Why do you apply pressure to a wound that is bleeding?

_____ 3. Why do you cover someone who is shivering?

_____ 4. Why do you keep a wound clean?

_____ 5. Why do you give someone with chest pains an aspirin?

_____ 6. Why do you keep a person who has a head injury from sleeping?

Answers

a. To avoid infection.

b. He or she may have a concussion.

c. He or she may be in shock.

d. Treatment for poison is different for different substances.

e. To stop the bleeding.

f. He or she may be having a heart attack and it could save their life.

B. Make a list of things you should have in a first-aid kit.

_____

_____

_____

_____

C. Write numbers next to each item in Exercise B, putting them in order of importance according to your opinion.

D. Study the chart.

Adverbial Clauses of Purpose and Manner		
Main clause	**Subordinate conjunction**	**Subordinate clause (dependent clause)**
You need to add pressure	so that	you can stop the bleeding.
Put your feet up	in order that	the blood goes to the heart and brain.
Keep medicines away from children	as	they could accidentally ingest it.
He is shivering	as if	he is in shock.
She looks	as though	she needs to lie down.
Some clauses of purpose or manner can go first and are offset from the main clause by a comma.		
As they can accidentally ingest it, keep medicine away from children.		
Subordinate adverbial clauses have a subject and verb construction, but they are dependent on the main clause for their meaning. Adverbial clauses of purpose or manner describe the purpose of the action in the main clause.		

E. Complete each statement with an adverbial clause from the box.

> in order that he can get a second opinion
> as if she has a headache
> ~~so that she can be there when her contractions get stronger~~
> as though she has never gotten a shot before
> as she will need her strength to make it though her physical therapy
> so that he can get his prescription filled

1. Call the doctor _so that she can be there when her contractions get stronger_____.

2. She is holding her head _____.

3. He wants to call the pharmacist _____.

4. He should call another doctor _____.

5. She needs to rest _____.

6. She is talking _____.

F. **Take the questions and answers from Exercise A and make complete statements.**

1. You should call a poison control center because treatment for poison is different for different substances.

2. _____

3. _____

4. _____

5. _____

6. _____

G. **Write sentences of advice for the situations below. Use adverbial clauses of purpose and manner.**

EXAMPLE: My hand is bleeding. You should clean it and cover it with a bandage so that it doesn't get infected.

1. My head is hurting. _____

_____

2. I feel dizzy. _____

_____

3. He is choking. _____

_____

4. She burned her hand. _____

_____

PRACTICE TEST

A. Read and circle the best answers.

Preventative Medicine

Many Americans ignore their health or think that they are healthy when they are not. It is amazing how many people have had heart attacks in the United States because they didn't get an annual check-up and were unaware of their overall health. Some people think doctors are only for sick people. They forget that preventative steps to safeguard their health can save their lives and maybe extend it by many years. Doctors may prescribe simple medications for lowering blood pressure or cholesterol. They will most likely also suggest exercise and a good diet for their patients. It's important to listen to your doctor in order to protect yourself against common diseases.

1. According to the reading passage, what has happened to some people who thought they were healthy and didn't get annual check-ups?
   a. They have developed high blood pressure.
   b. They have developed diabetes.
   c. They have had a heart attacks.
   d. They have developed common diseases.

2. Doctors are for . . .
   a. healthy people.
   b. sick people.
   c. old people.
   d. all of the above

3. The reading passage suggests that preventative steps can . . .
   a. extend your life.
   b. save your life.
   c. both a and b
   d. neither a nor b

4. What does the reading passage suggest you do to protect yourself against common diseases?
   a. listen to your doctor
   b. exercise
   c. eat healthy
   d. take medication

LESSON ① How much is it?

GOAL ■ Do product research

A. Discuss what you might consider when choosing where to shop. Add any additional considerations.

☐ store location

☐ store hours

☐ parking

☐ employees (salespeople and managers)

☐ _____

☐ _____

☐ product quality

☐ price

☐ service after purchase

☐ _____

☐ _____

☐ _____

B. Look at the list of considerations in Exercise A. What is most important to you? Put the considerations in order. *1* is the most important.

1. _____
2. _____
3. _____
4. _____
5. _____
6. _____
7. _____
8. _____
9. _____
10. _____
11. _____
12. _____

C. Study the chart.

	Adjective Clauses with Subject Pronouns	
	Adjective clause	**Clause construction**
Person (*who*)	She is the salesperson *who was in the store yesterday*. The salesperson *who was in the store yesterday* was excellent. (*Who* is the subject of the adjective clauses and modifies the preceding noun.)	**relative pronoun + verb** who was
Thing (*that* or *which*)	They bought the patio furniture *that was on sale*. The furniture, *which is on sale*, is beautiful. (*That* and *which* are the subjects of the adjective clauses and modify the preceding noun.)	that was which is
	Restrictive adjective clauses give essential information. **Example:** They bought the patio furniture *that was on sale*. This means there was some furniture that wasn't on sale and the clause specifies only the furniture on sale. Nonrestrictive adjective clauses give extra unnecessary information. Use commas to offset the clause and use *which* not *that* for things. **Example:** They bought the patio furniture, *which was on sale*. This means all the furniture was on sale and the information was not necessary to distinguish it from other furniture.	

D. Check (✓) the correct relative pronoun to complete each sentence.

	who	**that/which**
1. The store _____ I like best is far from my house.	☐	✓
2. The manager _____ runs that store says he'll match the price.	☐	☐
3. That product didn't come with the warranty _____ I wanted.	☐	☐
4. The woman _____ convinced me to buy it was nice.	☐	☐
5. I couldn't find the salesman _____ was helping me.	☐	☐
6. He bought the item _____ was the most expensive.	☐	☐
7. The speakers _____ came with a warranty were $700.	☐	☐

E. Look back at the sentences in Exercise D and separate each one into two sentences.

1. The store that I like best is far from my house.

   <u>I like that store best. The store is far from my house.</u>

2. _____

3. _____

4. _____

5. _____

6. _____

7. _____

F. Complete each sentence with an appropriate adjective clause.

1. The bed <u>that was the most comfortable</u> didn't come with a box spring.

2. The coupon _____ isn't good any more.

3. The manager _____ explained the warranty to us.

4. She wanted to buy the furniture _____.

5. They found a car _____.

6. The girl _____ said she would get the owner.

7. He read a book _____.

8. She researched the MP3 players _____.

G. Look at the list in Exercise A and write sentences about what is important to you in a shopping experience. Remember to use adjective clauses.

EXAMPLE: <u>The location of a store that I go to must be very close to my house.</u>

1. _____

2. _____

3. _____

4. _____

5. _____

6. _____

LESSON ② Shopping from home

GOAL ■ Purchase goods and services by phone and online

A. Answer the questions.

1. Do you get catalogs in the mail? If so, which ones?

   _____

2. Do you shop from catalogs? Why or why not?

   _____

3. What are the advantages of shopping from a catalog?

   _____

4. What are the disadvantages of shopping from a catalog?

   _____

5. Do you shop online? Why?

   _____

6. What are some things you can shop for online?

   _____

7. What are the advantages of shopping online?

   _____

8. What are the disadvantages of shopping online?

   _____

B. Look at each item and decide if you would prefer to buy it online, from a catalog, or in person.

1. computer	☐ online	☐ catalog	☐ in person
2. cell phone	☐ online	☐ catalog	☐ in person
3. book	☐ online	☐ catalog	☐ in person
4. sweater	☐ online	☐ catalog	☐ in person
5. toaster	☐ online	☐ catalog	☐ in person
6. violin	☐ online	☐ catalog	☐ in person
7. television	☐ online	☐ catalog	☐ in person
8. plant	☐ online	☐ catalog	☐ in person

C. Study the chart.

	Adjective Clauses with Object Pronouns				
	Adjective clause		**Clause construction**		
Person (*whom*)	She is the salesperson *whom I saw yesterday.* The salesperson *whom she spoke to* was excellent. (*Whom* is the object of the adjective clauses and modifies the preceding noun.)		relative pronoun + subject + verb whom whom	I she	saw spoke to
Thing (*that* or *which*)	They bought the patio furniture *that they found online.* The furniture, *which I saw on sale*, was beautiful. (*That* and *which* are the objects of the adjective clauses and modify the preceding noun.)		that which	they I	found saw
Reduced clauses: The relative pronoun can be deleted if it functions as an object. She is the salesperson (whom) I saw yesterday. They bought the patio furniture (that) they found online. Relative pronouns cannot be deleted if they follow prepositions. The salesperson to whom she spoke was excellent.					

D. Unscramble the adjective clauses.

1. will / contact / I / whom   _____whom I will contact_____

2. she / in class / whom / met   _____

3. she / that / buy / going to / is   _____

4. our friends / that / bought   _____

5. whom / like / you   _____

6. he / sold / which / me   _____

7. called / he / whom   _____

8. that / are / eat / you / going to   _____

9. which / have / they / at home   _____

10. commissioned / whom / we   _____

E. **Choose one of the adjective clauses you wrote in Exercise D to complete each sentence below.**

1. The person _____*whom I will contact*_____ is listed on the website.

2. She found the computer _____ in a catalog.

3. He sent me the watch _____ .

4. The students _____ buy all their clothes from catalogs.

5. The representative _____ helped him place his online order.

6. They bought the furniture _____ at an online auction.

7. We bought the fruit _____ at a farmers' market.

8. The artist _____ sells his work only in his gallery.

9. The car _____ retails for over $40,000.

10. The manager _____ is not working today.

F. **Complete each statement below with an adjective clause of your own.**

1. The stores _____*that I like to shop in*_____ are expensive.

2. These shoes _____ are killing my feet.

3. The girl _____ told me everything would be half price next week.

4. We bought some furniture _____ .

5. The salesman _____ said all the 2015 cars were on sale.

6. Carlos and his wife bought a new car _____ .

G. **Write two of your own sentences containing adjective clauses about a shopping experience.**

1. _____

2. _____

LESSON **3** Is this under warranty?

GOAL ■ Interpret product guarantees and warranties

A. A warranty and a guarantee are basically the same thing. Write a definition for the word *warranty*.

_____

_____

B. Think of products that you would need a warranty for and products you wouldn't need a warranty for. Make a list.

Warranty

_____

_____

_____

_____

No Warranty

_____

_____

_____

_____

C. Answer the questions.

1. When would you shop online instead of in a store?

_____

2. When would you use coupons?

_____

3. Why would you look for a product with a warranty?

_____

4. Why would you buy something at a garage sale or swap meet?

_____

5. What are the places where you like to shop for clothing? Groceries? Electronics?

_____

D. Study the chart.

Adjective Clauses Using *When*, *Where*, or *Why*		
	Adjective clause	**Clause construction**
Place	The store *where we bought the furniture* didn't offer a product guarantee. We bought a new guitar at a store *where they don't offer service guarantees*.	relative adverb + subject + verb where we bought where they don't offer
Time	We bought the computer on the day *when they were offering extended warranties*. She never thought she'd see the day *when you could buy things on the Internet*.	when they were offering when you could buy
Reason	The reason *why they didn't buy the printer* is it printed too slowly. Slow service is the reason *why we never shop at that store*.	why they didn't why we never shop
All adjective clauses have three essential components: 1) They contain a subject and a verb; 2) They begin with either a relative pronoun, *who, whom, whose, that,* or *which;* or a relative adverb, *where, when,* or *why;* and 3) They function as an adjective.		

E. Underline the adjective clause and circle the correct relative adverb in each statement.

1. Did you find a place (when /(where)/ why) they sell reusable bags?

2. The reason (when / where / why) I never shop at the supermarket is the fish isn't as fresh.

3. They went to a store (when / where / why) the salespeople work on commission.

4. Can we find a time (when / where / why) the mall is quiet and not crowded?

5. We buy our produce at a farm (when / where / why) they only grow vegetables.

6. I went looking for an umbrella on a day (when / where / why) it was raining.

7. He gave me a good explanation (when / where / why) that television didn't come with a warranty.

8. Her sister bought a restaurant (when / where / why) they used to serve Mexican food.

F. **Take each pair of sentences and combine them using the correct relative adverb. You may have to add a few words to ensure your new sentences make sense.**

1. I bought fabric. The store was having a sale.

   I bought the fabric when the store was having a sale.

2. We never go to the store on Sundays. It is crowded.

   _____

3. She bought her washing machine at a store. The store promised three years of free service.

   _____

4. I don't buy fish in the summer. The fish is not fresh.

   _____

5. We went on vacation to Mexico. It is hot in Mexico.

   _____

G. **For each of the nouns given, write an adjective clause using *when, where,* or *why.***

1. a store where they serve snacks while you shop _____

2. a time _____

3. a park _____

4. an afternoon _____

5. a place _____

H. **Look at the adjective clauses in Exercise G and use them to write complete sentences or questions.**

1. Have you ever been to a store where they serve snacks while you shop?

2. _____

3. _____

4. _____

5. _____

LESSON **4** **Returns and exchanges**

GOAL ■ Return a product

A. Read the refund policy.

> **Refund Policy:** The purchase must be returned in saleable condition. It must be in the original package and undamaged. No refunds or returns are permitted on opened software.
>
> All cash and check purchases will be refunded with cash provided that the purchase was made at the same store where the refund is requested. All credit card purchases will be refunded with a credit to the credit card used for the purchase. Refunds will only be made for purchases that are less than 14 days old. Any item over 14 days from purchase may be returned for store credit. A receipt is required with all refunds and returns. Exceptions to this policy are rare and can only be made by the store's general manager.

B. You are a salesclerk of a store with the above policy. Check (✓) what you would do in the following situations.

1. Monica purchased the stereo system a week ago. She used it for a week and now has to move. Her new apartment doesn't have room for the system. She wants to return it for a refund.

   ☐ Refund ☐ Store credit ☐ No return or refund ☐ Ask the manager

2. David purchased a new computer and used it for three days. It stopped working. He doesn't want to get it fixed through the warranty. He wants to return it and get his money back. He has the receipt, but he threw out the original packaging.

   ☐ Refund ☐ Store credit ☐ No return or refund ☐ Ask the manager

3. The guitar Jonathan purchased is new and hasn't been used at all. He purchased it as a gift for his girlfriend. She was disappointed and said she would prefer something different for her birthday. He purchased it five days ago. The store where he purchased it doesn't have anything but guitars.

   ☐ Refund ☐ Store credit ☐ No return or refund ☐ Ask the manager

C. **Study the rules for changing adjective clauses to adjective phrases.**

Rule	Adjective Clause to Adjective Phrase
Relative pronouns can be deleted if they function as objects. They cannot be deleted if they follow a preposition.	The salesperson (*whom*) I spoke to gave me a discount. The book (*that*) she bought can't be returned. The manager *to whom* I spoke solved the problem.
Relative pronouns can be deleted along with the *be* verb in the progressive or passive forms.	The store (*that is*) selling that book offers free bookmarks. He bought furniture (*that was*) made in Italy.
Relative pronouns can be deleted along with the *be* verb if they come before a preposition.	She found a bed (*that was*) on sale. Jason bought the guitar (*that was*) in the window.
A clause is a group of words that includes a subject and a verb. A phrase is a group of words that does not include a subject and a verb.	

D. **Cross out the unnecessary words in the adjective clauses below. Not all of the statements can be edited.**

1. The warranty ~~that is~~ offered by that store is the best one I have seen.

2. The salesperson whom he bought it from doesn't work there anymore.

3. Did you see the customer who was standing here a few minutes ago?

4. The stereo system that is playing right now is too big for Monica's new place.

5. The receipt that she has is too old.

6. I saw the patio furniture that was advertised in the paper.

7. Did they look for a house that was in their price range?

8. We never buy electronics that don't come with a warranty.

9. The new store that opened near our house is having a grand opening sale.

10. The couch that you sold me has fallen apart.

E. Complete each statement with the given adjective clause. Reduce the clauses if possible.

1. The products _____ *they sell* _____ don't appeal to us. (that they sell)

2. He found a deal _____. (that he couldn't pass up)

3. The salesperson _____ was very helpful. (whom he bought it from)

4. Shari is looking for a computer _____ a 3-year warranty. (that comes with)

5. She has searched every store _____. (that she could find)

6. Kenneth hopes to surprise his wife with the new washer and dryer _____. (that she has been wanting)

7. He found a set _____. (that comes with a free vacuum cleaner)

8. Hopefully, he can buy the ones _____. (that are on sale)

F. Write about a time when you had to return or exchange something. Include adjective clauses.

EXAMPLE: *The book (that) I bought was missing a page.*

_____

_____

_____

_____

_____

_____

_____

_____

_____

_____

LESSON **5** For sale

GOAL ■ Sell a product

A. Read the following announcements.

1. We, the English students at Jefferson Adult School, want to sell our old English textbooks for a discounted price.

2. The used TVs in our restaurant, selling for very cheap, will be available this Saturday only.

3. Our plan, to sell our antique furniture, tables, and chairs at an auction next week, is coming together.

4. That warehouse, the one with the blue door, will open to the public at 8 a.m.

B. Rewrite each announcement below without the phrase in the commas.

1. _____

2. _____

3. _____

4. _____

C. Look at what you wrote in Exercise B. Can you still understand the meanings of the sentences? Why?

_____

_____

D. **Study the chart.**

Appositives	
Appositives are nouns or noun phrases that rename nouns that they follow. There are three different types of appositives.	
Our financial advisor, *the woman whom our friends recommended to us*, suggests we put away money every month for retirement. The ad, *the one with all the great pictures*, shows how versatile the jacket can be.	noun phrase
Our plan, *shopping wisely*, helps us save money on everything we buy. Her idea, *buying the most expensive car*, will surely affect our budget.	gerund phrase
My goal, *to save as much money as I can*, will help us buy a car. His suggestion, *to read all of the ads*, will take us forever.	infinitive phrase

E. **Underline the appositive in each statement. After each statement, write the type of phrase:** *noun, gerund,* **or** *infinitive.*

1. Her new book, <u>the one with the red cover,</u> is selling like hotcakes. _____noun_____

2. My idea, to put ads in all the local papers, may cost more than I think it will. _____

3. His business, the website giving medical advice, isn't doing very well. _____

4. The used bike sale, happening every Wednesday, has drawn people from all over the state.

   _____

5. Our house, the brown one with the tiled roof, has been for sale for almost five months.

   _____

6. Jared's plan, to sell all of his furniture, is a great idea since he won't be moving back for

   at least two years. _____

7. Her wedding gown, the jeweled one with the pink lace, is not the prettiest wedding dress

   we have seen. _____

8. Her ad, the one with the artist's drawing, has been receiving a lot of attention. _____

9. The farmers' market, the one on State Street, only has farmers from local farms. _____

10. Her suggestion, to move all of the sale items into the window, was a great one. _____

F. **Write your own appositive phrases to complete each statement.**

1. His idea of fun, _buying plane tickets at an auction_, makes me nervous. (gerund)

2. The idea, _____, is really confusing. (infinitive)

3. Our children's clothing store, _____, will be soon offering shoes as well. (noun)

4. The stroller he is trying to sell, _____, is too old to get much money. (noun)

5. Her plan, _____, will surely work. (infinitive)

6. The sale, _____, should bring in a lot of money. (gerund)

G. **Think of three things you own that you would like to sell. Write statements using appositives.**

EXAMPLE: _My MP3 player, the newest one on the market, is for sale._

1. _____

2. _____

3. _____

H. **Now write announcements for the things you would like to sell, similar to the ones in Exercise A. Remember to use appositives.**

Announcement 1: _____

Announcement 2: _____

Announcement 3: _____

PRACTICE TEST

A. Read the conversation and choose the best answers.

Customer Service Representative (CSR): Can I help you?

Customer: Yes, I'm very unhappy with this computer.

CSR: What seems to be the trouble?

Customer: Everything! It doesn't even start most of the time.

CSR: I'm sure it can be fixed.

Customer: It's something that I don't want fixed. I want a new computer.

CSR: Well, I'm not sure we can do that.

Customer: Why not?

CSR: The manufacturer will have to help you, I think.

Customer: That's not good enough! Is there someone in charge who can help me?

CSR: I'll get the manager.

Customer: Thank you.

1. How do you think the customer is feeling?

   a. happy   b. frustrated

   c. bored   d. tired

2. Who is going to help the customer?

   a. the customer service representative   b. the manufacturer

   c. the manager   d. none of the above

3. What is the problem?

   a. The customer service representative can't fix the computer.   b. The manufacturer is unwilling to help.

                                       d. The customer is unhappy with her computer.

   c. The manager is unavailable.

4. What does the customer want?

   a. a new computer   b. her computer to be fixed

   c. technical support at her home   d. none of the above

GOAL ■ Identify and use technology

A. Read the introductory paragraph of the office handbook for Plano Distribution Center. Then, answer the questions.

> We would like to welcome you to the field services office of Plano Distribution Center. The office is the hub of our company. Your job is unique because we keep important and essential information in the office. This information is confidential and cannot be replaced. You are required to use the fax machines, computers, shredders, and copy machines every day, and you are to avoid using any of this equipment for personal use. We are a company of integrity, so if our personal files on clients were to reach our competitors, it would be devastating to our business. You have signed a letter of agreement stipulating your willingness to work under these conditions. The company has invested millions of dollars in the equipment you will use. This handbook will provide you with an orientation on using it. You will also receive training, and we will provide technical support when necessary.

1. Why is the job unique?

_____

2. What are employees required to do?

_____

B. A noun is a person, place, or thing. Look back at the paragraph in Exercise A and underline every noun you can find. How many did you find? _____

C. Put each noun you underlined into the appropriate column.

Person	Place	Thing
	office	

D. Study the chart.

Nouns: Pronouns, Phrases, and Clauses	
Definition	**Sample sentences**
Pronouns: words that take the place of nouns including subject pronouns, object pronouns, possessive pronouns, and reflexive pronouns	*It* is difficult. (subject) Javier loves *it*. (object) His computer is over there next to *mine*. (possessive) She sees *herself* in an office job in two years. (reflexive)
Noun Phrase: a group of words with a noun as the main word	*His job* is difficult. They need *three computers* for *the office*.
Noun Clause: a group of words that have a subject and verb. The clause may function as a noun. It can be the subject or object of a sentence	*What he does* is difficult. (subject) He loves *what he does*. (object)

E. Underline the noun phrases in the following sentences.

1. Your job is unique because we keep important and essential information in the office.

2. We would like to welcome you to the field services offices of Plano Distribution Center.

3. The office is the hub of our company.

4. You have signed a letter of agreement stipulating your willingness to work under these conditions.

5. We are a company of integrity, so if our personal files on clients were to reach our competitors, it would be devastating to our business.

F. Circle the pronouns in the following sentences.

1. You are required to use the fax machine.

2. We would like to welcome you to the field services offices of Plano Distribution Center.

3. This handbook with provide you with an orientation on using it.

4. Please make yourself familiar with it.

5. You will also receive training, and we will provide technical support when necessary.

G. Unscramble the noun clauses in each of the sentences below.

1. _____What you see_____ is exactly what you will be doing. (you / what / see)

2. The trainer explained exactly _____. (I / supposed / to do / was / what)

3. _____ was the key to the supply closet. (found / what / she)

4. _____ was how to run the copy machine. (learned / what / she)

5. She figured out _____. (she / what / to do / likes)

H. Complete each sentence below with a pronoun, a noun phrase, or a noun clause.

1. She finished _____the report_____.

2. _____ came and fixed the broken machine.

3. Could you help _____ figure this out?

4. I think I can do it by _____.

5. Did she ever learn how to operate _____?

6. _____ hope they will give _____ some time to study _____.

I. Write a sentence about each piece of technology. Use pronouns, noun phrases, or noun clauses in your sentences.

1. pedometer: _A pedometer is what you use to track your steps._____

2. scanner: _____

_____

3. tablet: _____

_____

4. smartphone: _____

_____

5. e-reader: _____

_____

LESSON ② How do you fix it?

GOAL ■ Resolve technology problems

A. Read the information in the table. Combine each problem and solution into a single sentence.

Problem	Solution
1. The secretary is concerned. The copy machine continually breaks down.	The manager asks the secretary to buy a new machine.
2. The secretary spoke to the manager. He sometimes treats the employees inappropriately.	The manager spoke with the secretary in private to understand her point of view and resolve the problem.
3. The secretary is interested in learning about new available software. She wants to hear what another employee has to say about it.	The manager set up a time for the employees to work together.
4. Several employees are on a committee to hire a new supervisor. They can't decide whom to hire.	The manager will make the decision.
5. The secretary went to the supply closet. The computer paper wasn't there.	The manager asks the secretary to complete a supply requisition.

1. _Because the secretary was concerned about the copy machine continually breaking down,_

the manager asked her to buy a new one.

2. _____

_____

3. _____

_____

4. _____

_____

5. _____

_____

B.   Study the chart.

Noun Clauses as Objects of the Preposition		
	Preposition	Noun clause = Object of the preposition
We are concerned	about	*what* she needs to do.
I am interested	in	*what* you have to say.
We can't decide	on	who we want for the new supervisor.
We went	to	where the paper was stored.
I spoke	about	how he treated other employees.
A noun clause as the object of a preposition starts with a question word and is followed by a subject and verb.		

C.   Choose a noun clause to complete each sentence. More than one may fit.

…where the meeting was held

~~…what he learned~~

…who would make a good leader

…who is giving the seminar

…where the conference is

…what she has to do next

…how to solve the problem

…what we can do to help

…how we can work together

1. She is interested in *what he learned* _____.

2. She came from _____.

3. We will need to think about _____.

4. She is concentrating on _____.

5. He is interested in _____.

6. I'm going to _____.

7. Our team needs to focus on _____.

8. His speech was about _____.

D. Use the expressions from Exercise C to complete the sentences.

1. _____We will need to think about_____ how often we can meet.

2. _____ where the new office will be.

3. _____ when the shipment will arrive.

4. _____ where the money was last seen.

5. _____ how to repair the printer.

6. _____ what we can do to divide our time.

E. Based on each problem, complete each sentence with a noun clause or an introduction to the noun clauses.

1. Problem: The copier is jammed.

   _____The technician is concerned about_____ how often the copier is jamming.

2. Problem: The printer is out of ink.

   _____ where to buy more ink.

3. Problem: My smartphone won't send e-mail.

   I am concerned about _____.

4. Problem: The scanner isn't reading the tickets.

   _____ what to do.

5. Problem: The tablet's screen is flashing.

   He isn't sure about _____.

6. Problem: The remote control for the television isn't working.

   Have you thought about _____?

F. Complete each statement about yourself with a noun clause.

1. I'm excited about _who I will meet in class_____.

2. I like to think about _____.

3. I'm going to figure out _____.

4. I used to focus on _____.

5. I want to learn about _____.

GOAL ■ Establish an organizational system

A. Read the evaluation about Sarah.

Employee Evaluation Form
Employee: Sarah Weinman **Supervisor:** Kirsten Malali   **Date:** October 27th
Sarah is a good worker. She is what I consider a model employee. I am particularly impressed by her organizational skills. She can find anything almost immediately; however, I am concerned that no one else may be able to understand her system. It seems that she works well in a team and people respect her. It seems that she can teach others. She has complained in the past about how we do certain things. I feel what she has to say has merit. **Suggestions for improvement:** 1. _____ 2. _____ **Supervisor's signature:** *Kirsten Malali* **Employee's signature:** *Sarah Weinman*

B. Answer the questions about the evaluation in Exercise A.

1. Would you say that this evaluation is mostly positive? Why?

    _____

    _____

2. What is the problem with Sarah's organizational system?

    _____

    _____

3. Sometimes Sarah complains. Do you think her complaints will have a positive or negative outcome? Why?

    _____

    _____

4. Write two suggestions for improvement on the form.

C. A verb is an action or describes a state of being. Look back at the evaluation in Exercise A and underline all the verbs that you can find.

D. Study the chart.

		Noun Clauses as Complements	
Subject	**Verb**	**Noun clause = Complement**	**Clause construction**
It	seems	*that they work together well as a team.*	*that* + subject + verb
They	are	*what we would call well organized.*	
She	became	*what they considered a problem in the office.*	
He	got	*what he wanted.*	*what* + subject + verb
You	felt	*what I said had merit, didn't you?*	
A complement always follows "to be," "to become," "to get," "to feel," or "to seem."			

E. Look at the sentences from Sarah's evaluation. For each sentence, write a sentence using noun clauses that indicates the opposite idea.

1. She is what I consider a model employee.

   _____

2. It seems that she works well in a team and people respect her.

   _____

3. I feel what she has to say has merit.

   _____

4. It seems that she can teach others.

   _____

5. I am particularly impressed by her organizational skills.

   _____

6. She has complained in the past about how we do certain things.

   _____

F. Unscramble the noun clauses.

1. she / that / her / job / likes

   _____ *that she likes her job* _____

2. see / I / like / to / what

   _____

3. what / hope / they / never / for / would

   _____

4. for / paid / what / he

   _____

5. she / that / harder / could / work

   _____

6. don't / to / like / very / they / hard / work / that

   _____

G. Choose a noun clause from Exercise F to complete each sentence below.

1. It seems _*that she likes her job*_____ .

2. It seems _____ .

3. She has become _____ .

4. That is _____ .

5. We all feel _____ .

6. He got _____ .

H. Write an evaluation for yourself. Use Sarah's evaluation in Exercise A as an example. Remember to use noun clauses.

_____

_____

_____

_____

_____

LESSON **4** **What's the problem?**

GOAL ■ Identify and resolve problems at work

A. **Read the summary of the conflict-resolution process.**

How employees and management resolve conflicts at work can make a difference in employee satisfaction. All people involved should follow a set process. Where they start is the most important issue. First, set ground rules, show mutual respect, and be willing to listen to all sides. This is called *setting the scene*. That everyone understands each other makes the process work better. Follow this by gathering information about the problem. What is next seems simple. Identify and agree upon the problem. Once people do this, they can brainstorm how to resolve the problem. The final step is to ensure everyone comes to a mutual agreement. The solution should be beneficial to all parties, but especially to the company.

B. **Write each step of the process in Exercise A in order.**

1. _____

2. _____

3. _____

4. _____

5. _____

C. **Take the situation below and decide how you would handle it following the steps in Exercise B.**

You are working in a team to create a product design. One of the team members isn't contributing. Instead he/she is writing personal e-mails, taking long breaks, and coming in late and leaving early.

_____

_____

_____

_____

_____

_____

_____

D. Study the chart.

Noun Clauses as Subjects		
Noun clause = Subject	**Verb**	
That our whole department got a raise	was	a surprise to us.
What we did yesterday	made	a big difference in office efficiency.
How she did her job	benefited	everyone.
Where I went	is	none of your business.
How they spoke to us	helped	me understand my job.
A noun clause as a subject of the verb starts with a question word or *that* and is followed by a subject and verb.		

E. Underline the noun clauses as subjects. Then, circle the main verbs.

1. Where you begin is the most important part of conflict resolution.

2. Where they start is the most important issue.

3. That everyone understands each other makes the process work better.

4. What is next seems simple.

5. What's important is identifying and agreeing upon the problem.

6. How you brainstorm can help you resolve the problem better.

7. That everyone comes to a mutual agreement is important.

8. What is important is that the solution is beneficial to all parties.

F. Complete each sentence with a noun clause.

1. _____How you react_____ can affect how the meeting will go.

2. _____ seems really difficult.

3. _____ is coming up with a valid solution.

4. _____ will force us to work together.

5. _____ makes it easier to get along.

6. _____ benefited the whole team.

7. _____ seems like the hardest part.

8. _____ can force us to work harder.

G. Imagine you are creating a classroom conflict-resolution manual. Write five statements using noun clauses to reflect your ideas.

EXAMPLE: _What is important is that we don't talk over one another._____

1. _____

2. _____

3. _____

4. _____

5. _____

H. How would you resolve the conflict below based on the ideas you wrote in Exercise G?

Javier has stolen the answers to the final exam. He has sold the answers to a few students in other classes for $20 each. You found out about it from a friend who is in another class.

_____

_____

_____

_____

_____

_____

LESSON **5** **What did you do?**

GOAL ■ Report progress

A. Read the progress report outline.

Project: Keyless Entry Project

- how much of the work is complete

  _____

- what part of the work is currently in progress

  _____

- what work remains to be done

  _____

- what problems or unexpected things, if any, have arisen

  _____

- how the project is going in general

  _____

B. Below is information about the Keyless Entry Project. Write the information below in the relevant sections in Exercise A.

☐ will complete a security scan of all employees, will train employees on keyless entry procedures and confidentiality

☐ re-keying the building and installing keyless entry system, starting a security scan of all employees, distributing key codes for keyless entry

☐ fair

☐ 80%

☐ contractor wants more money than he contracted for

C. Study the chart.

Noun Clauses as Objects of Verbs		
Subject + verb	**Noun clause**	**Explanation**
I did	*what* I was asked.	• A noun clause as an object of the verb starts with a question word or *that* and is followed by a subject and verb.
She knows	*how* to do a presentation.	
They decided	*where* the location would be.	
My boss asked	*who* would be best for the job.	• In this case, the noun clauses are the object of the sentence.
I hope	*that* they worked as a team.	

D. Answer each question with the noun clause given.

1. **Q:** What did you do?　　　　　**A:** (what she wanted me to)

   I did what she wanted me to.
   _____

2. **Q:** What does she hope?　　　　**A:** (that she will get some time off for all her hard work)

   _____

3. **Q:** What did he ask?　　　　　**A:** (how to complete the application form)

   _____

4. **Q:** What will we organize?　　　**A:** (what parts should go where)

   _____

5. **Q:** What do you know?　　　　**A:** (where the human resources office is)

   _____

6. **Q:** What are they going to decide?　　**A:** (how to divide the teams)

   _____

7. **Q:** What did you decide?　　　**A:** (what office I would work best in)

   _____

8. **Q:** What did she plan?　　　　**A:** (who would lead each part of the presentation)

   _____

E. Look out the outline in Exercise A and write sentences using noun clauses.

EXAMPLE: <u>I told him how much of the work is complete.</u>

1. _____

2. _____

3. _____

4. _____

F. Look at the to-do list below and write sentences using noun clauses.

Date: July 11th		TO-DO LIST		
Completed	Priority 1–3	Action item	Decided by whom	Time promised
☐	_____	Reorganize files	me	8:30 a.m.
☐	_____	Make copies for board meeting	supervisor	4:00 p.m.
☐	_____	Set appointments for new hires	supervisor	4:00 p.m.
☐	_____	Write letters for sales reps	sales reps	4:00 p.m.
☐	_____	Have fax machine fixed	office staff	12:00 p.m.
☐	_____	Have lunch with Bill	me	ongoing
☐	_____	Train new office staff	manager	ongoing
☐	_____	Answer customer phone calls	sales reps	4:00 p.m.
☐	_____	Complete call log	reps/supervisor	4:00 p.m.
☐	_____	Send thank-you notes to staff	me	

EXAMPLE: <u>I will decide where to have lunch with Bill.</u>

1. _____

2. _____

3. _____

4. _____

5. _____

6. _____

PRACTICE TEST

A. Read the conversation and choose the best answers.

Employee:　Excuse me, sir, may I ask you a few questions?

Supervisor:　Sure, please come in and sit down.

Employee:　I understand that there will be budget cuts this year.

Supervisor:　Yes, that's right, but we don't know yet if any jobs will be cut.

Employee:　I really wanted to discuss if I am doing a good job or if I need to worry.

Supervisor:　You are doing a great job, but I still can't say whether or not that matters. It is up to the owner of the company.

Employee:　Thank you for being honest with me. Let me ask you one more question.

Supervisor:　No problem.

Employee:　I am curious whether or not it would be a good idea to look for another job, and if you can give me a letter of recommendation or not.

Supervisor:　Please wait another month. I will hopefully have answers for you by then. We would hate to lose you.

Employee:　Thank you, sir. I will consider it.

1. Who is part of the conversation?

   a. employee, owner, and supervisor　　　　b. employee and supervisor

   c. employee and owner　　　　　　　　　　d. supervisor and owner

2. What is the employee concerned about?

   a. budget cuts　　　　　　　　　　　　　b. looking for a new job

   c. losing his/her job　　　　　　　　　　d. talking to the owner

3. What does the supervisor suggest he/she does?

   a. look for a new job　　　　　　　　　　b. talk to the owner

   c. talk to other employees about　　　　d. wait
      the budget cuts

4. What does the supervisor say to make you think he/she is a good employee?

   a. "We don't know if any jobs will be cut."　　b. "Please wait another month."

   c. "We would hate to lose you."　　　　　　d. "It is up to the owner of the company."

LESSON **1** Investigating citizenship

GOAL ■ Identify requirements for establishing residency and citizenship

A. Read the paragraph below and answer the questions.

Many people consider being a citizen of the United States a privilege. Certainly, citizens have specific rights. An immigrant who wants to become a citizen must establish himself or herself in the United States, learn English, and follow all the laws of the land. Since the laws for citizenship in other countries may be different from those of the United States, some people can have dual citizenship, meaning they can be citizens of the United States and another country at the same time. When a person takes the steps necessary to become a citizen and when all requirements are met, he or she takes an oath stating a willingness to obey the laws and support the country. This person is then known as a naturalized citizen and has all the rights of someone born in the country.

1. What is a naturalized citizen?

   _____

   _____

2. What is dual citizenship?

   _____

   _____

3. According to the reading passage, what are the three requirements to become a citizen of the United States?

   a. _____

   b. _____

   c. _____

4. What is the purpose of the oath?

   _____

   _____

B. Underline all the nouns in the paragraph.

C. **Study the chart.**

Articles: *A*, *An*, and *The*		
Rules (article + noun)	**Example**	**What it means**
a or an Use *a* or *an* when the noun that follows represents one of a class of things or when the sentence is making a generalization. *An* is used when the noun that follows starts with a vowel sound.	*A citizen* has specific rights.	*A citizen* = any citizen or just citizens in general. Sometimes the speaker means all citizens
the Use *the* when the listener and the speaker both have the same specific idea in mind represented by the noun.	*The citizen* we spoke about yesterday has his rights.	*The citizen* = a specific person who has already been identified
Note: Singular count nouns must be preceded by an article, this/that, or a possessive adjective.		

D. **Underline all of the articles in the sentences below and write the reasons why they are used.**

1. Many people consider being <u>a</u> citizen of the United States a privilege.

   Reason: _a citizen in general_

2. An immigrant who wants to become a citizen must establish himself or herself in the United States, learn English, and follow all the laws of the land.

   Reason: _____

3. When a person takes the steps necessary to become a citizen and when all requirements are met, he or she takes an oath stating a willingness to obey the laws and support the country.

   Reason: _____

4. This person is then known as a naturalized citizen and has all the rights of someone born in the country.

   Reason: _____

E. Fill in each blank with an appropriate article.

1. ___The___ green card I have been waiting for finally came in ___the___ mail.

2. Salwa is _____ refugee from the Middle East. _____ country she comes from doesn't allow emigration.

3. Ella is 35, and her mother just became _____ permanent resident.

4. Marna just got _____ green card. _____ card came in the mail yesterday.

5. Have you taken _____ citizenship test?

6. _____ citizenship class they offer at my school starts at _____ beginning of _____ month.

7. He took _____ oath last week and is now _____ naturalized citizen.

8. She wants to apply to become _____ citizen but doesn't know what steps to take.

9. Her daughter was born in _____ United States so she is a citizen. But her father is still waiting to become _____ permanent resident.

10. Jared and his brother are trying to come to _____ United States for _____ job. They are hoping _____ company that wants to hire them will sponsor them.

F. Write a paragraph about someone you know who has gone through the citizenship process.

_____

_____

_____

_____

_____

_____

G. Underline the articles in your paragraph in Exercise F. Did you use the right ones?

LESSON ② Rights

GOAL ■ Understand your rights

A. Read a summary of the *amendments* in the *Bill of Rights*.

1. Freedom of religion, speech, press, assembly, and petition
2. Freedom to bear arms
3. No quartering of soldiers
4. Freedom from unreasonable searches and seizures
5. Freedom from unlawful imprisonment
6. Right to a speedy and public trial
7. Right to trial by jury
8. Freedom from unusual punishment
9. Other rights of the people
10. Powers reserved to the states

B. Read the situations. Identify the amendment you think is involved.

1. John has been accused of a crime. He is innocent and insists that he have a trial immediately

   to prove his innocence. _____

2. John has a permit to own a gun and keeps it in his home for protection. _____

3. John disagrees with the judge in his case and writes a letter to the newspaper. They

   publish it. _____

C. Study the chart.

Definite Articles vs. Nothing (Ø)		
Rules (article + noun)	**Example**	**What it means**
the Use *the* when the listener and the speaker both have the same specific idea in mind represented by the noun.	**The** *rights* that citizens have include the right to vote.	*The rights* = rights specified in the U.S. Constitution
Ø (no article) Use no article with plural nouns when making generalizations.	*Citizens* have specific rights.	*Citizens* = any citizen or just citizens in general. Sometimes the speaker means all citizens
Ø (no article) Use no article with noncount nouns when making generalizations.	*Justice* is another word for *fairness* under the law.	*Justice and fairness* = generalizations that cannot be counted
Ø (no article) Use no article with proper names unless the article is part of the name (*the United States of America*).	*Judge Harvey Spanner* declared his support for the new mayor.	*Judge Harvey Spanner* = the name of the judge

Note: Singular count nouns must be preceded by an article, *this/that*, or a possessive adjective.

D. Underline the nouns in the following sentences. Which ones have articles or a word modifying the noun? Why? Which ones don't have articles? Why not?

1. The <u>residents</u> of her <u>town</u> called several town hall <u>meetings</u>.

2. People want to change the immigration system.

3. Candidates always promise more than they can deliver.

4. Do you think fairness was involved in his decision?

5. Dr. Stevens presented his paper on global warming.

6. The classes that we took prepared us to pass the interview.

E. Complete each statement with the noun given. If necessary, put *the* in front of the noun.

1. (citizens) _____The citizens_____ of California recalled their governor.

2. (happiness) _____ is something you can't put a price on.

3. (refugees) _____ from Vietnam settled in communities together.

4. (problems) We have found _____ with the green card system.

5. (crimes) _____ committed in that town are worse than those committed in other nearby towns.

6. (documents) He sent _____ I had been waiting for.

7. (belongings) The Fourth Amendment guarantees that _____ are protected from search and seizure.

8. (soldiers) _____ are brave.

9. (justice) Do you think that _____ was served?

10. (Senator Lyons) _____ voted against the bill.

F. Write statements based on the summary of the amendments in Exercise A. Start each sentences with *The Bill of Rights guarantees* .... Remember to use the definite article.

EXAMPLE: _The Bill of Rights guarantees the freedom of religion, speech, press, assembly, and petition._

1. _____

_____

2. _____

_____

3. _____

_____

4. _____

_____

5. _____

_____

GOAL ■ Identify local civic organizations

A.   Read about the Hamilton Club.

> The Hamilton Club was established in 1965. It is a service organization with 3,200 members worldwide. The club helps provide food to underprivileged families. This organization is proud of the efforts made over the past forty years. To become a member of Hamilton, you must . . .
>
> 1) be willing to contribute to underprivileged families.
> 2) attend monthly meetings.
> 3) take leadership roles in the club.

B.   Underline the words that refer to the Hamilton Club in the reading passage in Exercise A.

C.   Would you want to be part of a club like this? Why?

_____

_____

_____

D.   Imagine you are creating your own club. Complete the outline below.

Club name: _____

Purpose of club: _____

Number of members: _____

Type of members: _____

To become a member you must _____

_____

_____

_____

E. Study the charts.

Rules	Examples	
Repetition: Referent can be repeated as originally stated or parts of it can be repeated.	*The Hamilton Club* is a service organization. It has a long history. *The Club* was established in 1965.	*The Hamilton Club* is repeated in a shortened form (*The club*).
Synonym: Referent can be repeated as another word.	*The organization* is a service organization. *The group* was established in 1965.	*The group* is a synonym for the referent, which is *the organization*.
Classifier: A demonstrative determiner followed by a noun that classifies the referent is called a classifier.	*The Hamilton Club* is very interested in service. *This organization was* established in 1965.	*The Hamilton Club* has been classified as an organization here.
Paraphrase: The referent can be a process. When this is the case, the process can be given a new name usually preceded by *this*.	To join the Hamilton Club, you must be recommended by a member and then go through a ceremony. *This initiation* is a simple process.	*This initiation* refers to the process of becoming a member of the Hamilton Club.

Definitions	Example	
Referent = a familiar word that is referred to later in a passage	The Hamilton Club is a service organization. *It* was established in 1965.	*It* refers back to the referent, which is *the Hamilton Club*.
Demonstrative determiners = *this, that, these, those* Determiners combine with nouns.	The Hamilton Club is a service organization. *This* organization has over 3,200 clubs throughout the world.	*This organization* refers to *the Hamilton Club*.

F. Underline the referents to the Boys Club in the following statements.

1. <u>The club</u> was established in 1989.

2. It meets twice a month.

3. The organization only allows boys age 11 and older to join.

4. All members of the group must pay $45 annually.

5. The organization doesn't discriminate.

6. It is very inclusive.

G. Complete the paragraph about The Mother's Club with the words and phrases from the box. Use a different phrase in each blank.

~~The Mother's Club~~	the club	the organization
a group	The Mother's Club	the club's

___The Mother's Club___ (1) is a group of 35 dynamic women working to help Northville

schoolchildren excel by providing enrichment opportunities. In 1935, _____

(2) of 12 women decided to meet regularly for enlightenment and social activities. During

the Depression of the 1930s, _____ (3) held a fundraiser to purchase milk for

schoolchildren to drink with their lunches. _____ (4) fundraising has now grown

to three events each year, enabling them to donate approximately $30,000 annually to student

enrichment programs and activities. _____ (5) performs service projects at the

public school buildings on a rotating cycle, working at two or three schools each year. As far as

social events, _____ (6) has book club meetings once a month and lunch and

movie afternoons twice a year.

H. Complete the following paragraph with your own referent phrases.

Five years ago, a group of friends who wanted to learn more about the stock market got together

and started an investment club. They call themselves the Bond Boys. _____ (1) meets

once a month online and face-to-face twice a year. The purpose of _____ (2) is to

learn while investing their money in stocks for the long term. _____ (3) runs like a

club with officers. Each member of _____ (4) pays $100 a month in dues. That money

is then invested in whatever stock _____ (5) decides upon. _____

(6) has a lot of fun while learning at the same time.

I. Use the ideas you came up with in Exercise D and write a paragraph on a separate piece of paper describing your club. Remember to use a range of referents.

LESSON **4** Saving the environment

GOAL ■ Interpret information about environmental issues

A. **Look at the suggestions for creating less trash. Check the five items you think are easiest to do.**

> ### Create Less Trash
>
> ☐ Buy items in bulk from loose bins when possible to reduce wasted packaging.
>
> ☐ Avoid products with several layers of packaging when only one is sufficient.
>
> ☐ Buy products that you can reuse.
>
> ☐ Maintain and repair durable products instead of buying new ones.
>
> ☐ Check reports for products that are easily repaired and have low breakdown rates.
>
> ☐ Reuse items like bags and containers when possible.
>
> ☐ Use cloth napkins instead of paper ones.
>
> ☐ Use reusable plates and utensils instead of disposable ones.
>
> ☐ Use reusable containers to store food instead of aluminum foil and cling wrap.
>
> ☐ Shop with a canvas bag instead of using paper and plastic bags.
>
> ☐ Buy rechargeable batteries for devices used frequently.
>
> ☐ Reuse packaging cartons and shipping materials. Old newspapers make great packaging material.
>
> ☐ Buy used furniture—there is a surplus of it, and it is much cheaper than new furniture.

B. **Which five suggestions do you think help the environment the most?**

1. _____

2. _____

3. _____

4. _____

5. _____

C. Study the chart.

Demonstratives Determiners		
	Singular	**Plural**
Near	this	these
Far	that	those

Demonstratives determiners (or adjectives) tell the reader if the noun is near or far and singular or plural. **Demonstrative pronouns** represent a noun that is near or far and singular or plural. Nouns can be omitted if referred to previously.

	Examples	
Near (space)	This (trash can) is used for recycling.	The trash can is near the speaker.
Far (space)	That (trash can) is used for recycling.	The trash can is not within reaching distance of the speaker.
Near (time)	These (recycling systems) we learned about are great.	They learned about the recycling system a short time ago, probably the same day.
Far (time)	Those (recycling systems) we learned about are great.	They learned about the recycling system previously.

D. Underline the demonstratives in each statement. Then decide if the demonstratives are indicating near or far. Write *near* or *far* on the lines.

1. <u>These</u> bottles are recyclable. _____near_____

2. Those napkins are cloth so we should use them. _____

3. Can these batteries be recharged? _____

4. Those suggestions we learned for creating less trash are really useful. _____

5. This maintenance plan is difficult to understand. _____

6. Those products in bulk from the market are a great deal! _____

7. This furniture is used, and it was so much cheaper than the new stuff we looked at. _____

8. Where did you get these reusable bags? _____

9. Why does the box need all those layers of packaging? _____

10. Did you see that report on those new products? _____

E. Complete each statement with *this, that, these,* or *those* based on the information given.

1. _____Those_____ washers are very efficient and use a very small amount of energy. (far)

2. How long have you had _____ water heater? (near)

3. Please don't open _____ oven door while the chicken is cooking. (far)

4. Did you wash _____ clothes with hot water or cold? (near)

5. She put _____ insulated blanket around her water heater. (near)

6. Do you know what temperature _____ refrigerator is set at? (near)

7. I replaced _____ filter on our air-conditioning unit. (far)

8. We always unplug _____ appliances before we go away on vacation. (near)

9. _____ filter in our dryer is always full of lint. (far)

10. He always leaves _____ lights on! (far)

F. Write four statements about things you do that are good for the environment. Remember to use demonstratives.

EXAMPLE: *I use this container to hold my recyclables.*

1. _____

2. _____

3. _____

4. _____

G. Write a list of ways to conserve water. Remember to use demonstratives.

1. _____

2. _____

3. _____

4. _____

5. _____

6. _____

GOAL ■ Communicate your opinion

A. Read one person's opinion on the advantages and disadvantages of carpooling.

Advantages to carpooling	Disadvantages to carpooling
Expense: Share the expenses (car maintenance and gas) with others who drive. Your insurance will be cheaper, too.	Expense: Family emergencies, outside lunch appointments, or unexpected overtime may require making other, sometimes costly arrangements.
Stress: In busy areas, driving can be very stressful. Sharing the driving responsibilities can reduce stress.	Stress: Sometimes those you are commuting with have bad habits, talk too much, don't talk enough, or complain about your driving.
Pollution and Congestion: Fewer cars because of carpoolers means less pollution caused by motor vehicles.	Pollution and Congestion: In places with few cars and where commute time is very short, the advantages don't outweigh the disadvantages.
Convenience: People who work together and have the same work schedule can carpool. If the boss wants you to finish a project before you leave, you have a good excuse to leave it for tomorrow.	Convenience: Many people have varied work schedules that change regularly, they like to do errands on the way home or to work, and their car is available in case of emergency.
Time: The carpool or HOV (high occupancy vehicle) lane allows you to travel faster.	Time: Your starting and returning time is restricted to the people you carpool with.

B. Would carpooling work for you? Explain your reasons why.

_____

_____

_____

_____

_____

_____

C. Study the chart.

<table>
<tr><th colspan="3">Such and Demonstrative Determiners</th></tr>
<tr><th></th><th>Examples</th><th></th></tr>
<tr>
<td>this + noun
Use this with singular nouns that represent specific things.</td>
<td>Her opinion is that we should all carpool. Is this opinion really based on reality?</td>
<td>This refers to the specific opinion that everyone should carpool.</td>
</tr>
<tr>
<td>such a(n) + noun
Use such a(n) with singular nouns that represent classes or subgroups of the nouns.</td>
<td>Her opinion is that we should all carpool. Is such an opinion really based on reality?</td>
<td>Such an is referring to any opinion like the one mentioned and not only the opinion that everyone should carpool.</td>
</tr>
<tr>
<td>these + noun
Use these with plural nouns that represent specific things.</td>
<td>The carpool lanes that have walls on either side can be dangerous when there are accidents. These lanes are also difficult to merge in and out of.</td>
<td>These lanes refer to all carpool lanes.</td>
</tr>
<tr>
<td>such + noun
Use such with plural nouns that represent classes or groups that have been specified.</td>
<td>The carpool lanes that have walls on either side can be dangerous when there are accidents. Such lanes are also difficult to merge in and out of.</td>
<td>Such lanes refer to only the carpool lanes with walls on either side.</td>
</tr>
<tr>
<td colspan="3">Use this or such with noncount nouns. Use this for specific and such for general.</td>
</tr>
</table>

D. Complete all of the A statements with *this* or *these* and all of the B statements with *such a/an* or *such*.

1. They stopped driving completely to save money on gas.

   A. Is _____ situation really true?

   B. Is _____ situation possible in a suburban neighborhood?

2. Some car companies are making more hybrid vehicles.

   A. _____ vehicles are more expensive than the non-hybrid versions.

   B. _____ vehicles could help save the environment.

3. Many gas stations are offering gas incentives.

   A. Will _____ incentives really work?

   B. Will _____ incentives really work?

E. **Respond to each statement with your own opinion. Your opinion can be specific or general.**

EXAMPLE: One company is trying to bring back the electric car.

Such innovations will surely help our environment.

1. Carpooling is a waste of time.

_____

2. You should try to walk instead of driving your car.

_____

3. Public transportation is a great way to get around.

_____

4. It is impossible for parents of small children not to be driving all over the place.

_____

5. Smaller cars are just as bad for the environment as bigger ones.

_____

F. **Use your ideas from Exercise B to state your opinions about carpooling. Remember to use demonstrative determiners and _such_.**

_____

_____

_____

_____

_____

_____

PRACTICE TEST

A. Read and choose the best answers.

> There are many ways we can protect the world we live in, but one of the most important things we can do is conserve water. Why? Water is our most precious resource. First of all, the human body is made up of 75% water. We could only live for one week without water; therefore, we need to drink it to survive. Another reason that water is so important is that we need it to clean. We need water to clean our bodies, wash dishes, and launder clothes. Still another reason is that plants and trees need water to grow and survive. Without plants and trees, humans wouldn't survive because plants give off oxygen that we need in order to breathe. For these reasons, I believe that we need to conserve our most precious resource—water.
>
> Conserving water is simple: Take a shorter shower, put more clothes in a load of washing, fill up the dishwasher before you run it, turn off the water while you are brushing your teeth, water your plants less often, don't use a hose to clean your patio and yard. Simple, right? Following these simple ideas could make a big difference. So please do your part in trying to help save our planet.

1. The author believes that _____ is our most important resource.

   a. plants

   b. water

   c. trees

   d. all of the above

2. Why is water so important?

   a. It helps plants and trees survive.

   b. We need to drink it to survive.

   c. We need water to clean.

   d. all of the above

3. What is NOT a way the author suggests to save water?

   a. Turn off the water while you are taking a shower.

   b. Water your plants less often.

   c. Fill the dishwasher and washing machine before you use them.

   d. Don't use a hose to clean your patio.

4. How many reasons does the author give for why water is our most precious resource?

   a. 1   b. 2   c. 3   d. 4

GLOSSARY OF GRAMMAR TERMS

adjective	a word that describes a noun (Example: the _red_ hat)
adverb	a word that modifies a verb, adjective, or another adverb (Example: She eats _quickly_.)
affirmative	not negative and not a question (Example: _I like him._)
apostrophe	a punctuation mark that shows missing letters in contractions or possession (Example: _It's_ or _Jim's_)
article	words used before a noun (Example: _a_, _an_, _the_)
base form	the main form of a verb, used without _to_ (Example: _be_, _have_, _study_)
comma	a punctuation mark used to indicate a pause or separation (Example: I live in an apartment, and you live in a house.)
complement	a word or words that add to or complete an idea after the verb (Example: He is _happy_.)
conjugation	the form of a verb (Example: I _am_, You _are_, We _are_, They _are_, He _is_, She _is_, It _is_)
continuous form	a verb form that expresses action during time (Example: He _is shopping_.)
contraction	shortening of a word, syllable, or word group by omission of a sound or letter (Example: It is = _It's_, does not = _doesn't_)
count nouns	nouns that can be counted by number (Example: one _apple_, two _apples_)
definite article	use of _the_ when a noun is known to speaker and listener (Example: I know _the_ store.)
exclamation mark	a punctuation symbol marking surprise or emotion (Example: Hello_!_)
formal	polite or respectful language (Example: _Could_ you _please_ give me that?)
imperative	a command form of a verb (Example: _Listen_! or _Look out_!)
indefinite article	_a_ or _an_ used before a noun when something is talked about for the first time or when _the_ is too specific (Example: There's _a_ new restaurant.)
infinitive	the main form of a verb, usually used with _to_ (Example: I like _to run_ fast.)
informal	friendly or casual language (Example: _Can_ I have that?)
irregular verb	a verb different from regular form verbs (Example: be = _am, are, is, was, were, being_)
modal auxiliary	a verb that indicates a mood (ability, possibility, etc.) and is followed by the base form of another verb (Example: I _can read_ English well.)
modifier	a word phrase that describes another (Example: a _good_ friend)
negative	the opposite of affirmative (Example: She _does not_ like meat.)
noun	a name of a person, place, or thing (Example: _Joe, England, bottle_)
noncount nouns	nouns impossible or difficult to count (Example: _water, love, rice, fire_)

object, direct	the focus of a verb's action (Example: I eat <u>*oranges*</u>.)
object pronoun	replaces the noun taking the action (Example: *Julia* is nice. I like <u>*her*</u>.)
past tense	a verb form used to express an action or state in the past (Example: You <u>*worked*</u> yesterday.)
period	a punctuation mark ending a sentence (.)
plural	indicating more than one (Example: *pencil<u>s</u>, child<u>ren</u>*)
possessive adjective	an adjective expressing possession (Example: <u>*our*</u> car)
preposition	a word that indicates relationship between objects (Example: <u>*on*</u> the *desk*)
present tense	a verb tense representing the current time, not past or future (Example: They <u>*are*</u> at home right now.)
pronoun	a word used in place of a noun (Example: *Ted* is 65. <u>*He*</u> is retired.)
question form	to ask or look for an answer (Example: <u>*Where is my book?*</u>)
regular verb	verb with endings that are regular and follow the rule (Example: work = *work, work<u>s</u>, work<u>ed</u>, work<u>ing</u>*)
sentence	a thought expressed in words, with a subject and verb (Example: <u>*Julia works hard*</u>.)
short answer	a response to a *yes/no* question, usually a subject pronoun and auxiliary verb (Example: <u>*Yes, I am*</u>, or <u>*No, he doesn't*</u>.)
singular	one object (Example: <u>*a cat*</u>)
statement	a sentence or thought (Example: <u>*The weather is rainy today*</u>.)
subject	the noun that does the action in a sentence (Example: <u>*The gardener works*</u> here.)
subject pronoun	a pronoun that takes the place of a subject (Example: *John* is a sudent. <u>*He*</u> is smart.)
syllable	a part of a word as determined by vowel sounds and rhythm (Example: <u>*ta-ble*</u>)
tag questions	short informal questions that come at the end of sentences in speech (Example: You like soup, <u>*don't you?*</u> They aren't hungry, <u>*are they?*</u>)
tense	the part of a verb that shows the past, present, or future time (Example: He *talk<u>ed</u>*.)
verb	word describing an action or state (Example: The boys <u>*walk*</u> to school. I <u>*am*</u> tired.)
vowels	the letters <u>*a, e, i o, u,*</u> and sometimes *y*
wh- questions	questions that ask for information, usually starting with *Who, What, When, Where,* or *Why*. (Example: <u>*Where*</u> do you live?) *How* is often included in this group.
yes/no questions	questions that ask for an affirmative or a negative answer (Example: *Are you happy?*)

GRAMMAR REFERENCE

Gerunds as Objects of Prepositions			
Verb	**Preposition**	**Gerund**	**Example sentence**
learn learn best	by	writing participating	He **learns by writing** everything down. They **learn best by participating** in a discussion.
learn	through by	repeating watching	They **learn through listening**.
practice	by	relating solving	We **practice by repeating** what we hear. I **practice by watching** a video.
(be) good	at	remembering	Logical learners **are good at solving** problems.
excel succeed	in in	taking listening	You **excel in remembering** information. I **succeed in taking** good notes.
struggle	with	identifying	That student **struggles with listening** in class.

Gerunds as Direct Objects			
Verb	**Infinitive or Gerund**	**Example sentence**	**Other verbs that follow the same rule**
want plan	+ infinitive	He **wants to study** art. He **planned to learn** English.	arrange, choose, decide, expect, hope, prepare, resolve
enjoy finish	+ gerund	She **enjoys fixing** cars. She **finished studying** for the test.	anticipate, consider, complete, discuss, imagine, necessitate, recommend
like	+ infinitive or + gerund	They **like to paint**. We **like painting**.	begin, commence, continue, love, prefer, try

infinitive = *to* + verb
gerund = verb + *ing*

Simple Past/Present Perfect/Simple Present		
Simple Past	Something that started and ended in the past.	Juan was born in 1989.
Present Perfect	Something that started in the past and continues in the present.	Juan has been in the United States for three years.
Present	Something that is true about the present.	Juan works in a department store.
Future	Something that will happen in the future.	He is going to / will study architecture in college.

Simple Tenses

Subject	Past	Present	Future	
I	spent	spend	will spend	more time with my brothers.
You	enjoyed	enjoy	will enjoy	being a mother.
He, She, It	studied	studies	will study	English every day.
We	put	put	will put	our studies first.
They	worked	work	will work	too many hours.

Be

Subject	Past	Present	Future
I	was	am	will be
You	were	are	will be
He, She, It	was	is	will be
We	were	are	will be
They	were	are	will be

Past Perfect

Subject	Had/Hadn't	Past participle	Complement	Clause
I, He, She, We, You, They	had hadn't	**trained**	for six months	before I ran the marathon
		(already) **taken**	English classes	when I started college
		studied	at the university	I went to medical school*

*After **I had studied** at the university, **I went** to medical school.

• The past perfect can show an event that happened before another event in the past.
• The past perfect can show that something happened before the verb in the *when* clause.
*The past perfect can show something that happened after another event. In this case the *after* clause includes the past perfect and the clauses are separated with a comma.

Future Perfect Tense

Subject	Will Have	Past participle		Second future event (present tense)
I	**will have**	**become**	a teacher	by the time my kids are in school.
He	**will have**	**been**	a graphic designer (for five years)	when he turns 35.
They	**will have**	**found**	a job	by the time I finish school.

• We use the future perfect to talk about an activity that will be completed before another time or event in the future. **Note:** The order of events is not important. If the second future event comes first, use a comma.
By the time my kids are in school, I will have become a teacher.

Future Perfect Continuous: *Will have been* + Verb + *ing*

Example sentence	Duration	Future event or action
She **will have been studying** architecture for three years by the time she gets her degree.	three years	gets her degree
They **will have been working** at the same job for twenty years when they retire.	twenty years	retire

- Use the *future perfect continuous* to emphasize **the duration** of an activity that leads up to a future time or event.

Note: The *future perfect* is used in a similar way, but it doesn't emphasize duration.

Future Perfect Tense

Completed future event	Second future event
I **will have saved** $3,000	by the time he arrives.
You **will have paid** off the house	when you reach retirement.
They **will have found** jobs	by the time they finish school.

We use the **future perfect** to talk about an activity that will be completed before another time or event in the future.

Past Perfect Continuous Tense

First past activity					Second past event
Subject	*Had*	*Been*	*-ing* verb		Simple past
Sheila	**had**	**been**	**buying**	designer clothes	before she started bargain shopping.
Sam	**had**	**been**	**making**	coffee at home	before he began buying it at a coffee shop.
They	**had**	**been**	**paying**	a higher deductible	before they called the insurance company.

We use the past perfect continuous to talk about an activity that was happening for a while before another event that happened in the past. For the more recent event, we use the simple past.

Modals: *Can* and *Could* (Ability)

Subject	Modal	Base	Complement
I, You, He, She, It, We, They	**can** **could**	save invest spend	our money my savings his earnings

- Use *can* as a modal to express ability or what is possible to do. Use *could* with the same verb to express a suggestion or a possibility.
  - We can invest our money in a CD. (expresses ability)
  - We could invest our money in a CD. (expresses ability but only as a suggestion)

Modals: *Should* and *Ought to* (Advisability)

Subject	Modal	*have* + participle	Complement
I, You, He, She, It, We, They	**should** **ought to**	have looked	for errors
		have checked	our credit report

- Use *should* or *ought to* interchangeably. When used with *have* and the past participle, they express advice about something done in the past.

Modals: *May, Might,* and *Could* (Uncertainty)

Subject	Modal	*have* + participle	Complement
It	**may** **might** **could**	have gotten	stolen online
Someone, He, She, They		have found	your social security number
It		have been	identity theft

- Use modals like *may, might,* and *could* with *have* and the past participle to describe possibility or uncertainty in something that happened in the past.
  It could have been identity theft. (The speaker doesn't know. He or she is expressing the possibility. He or she is uncertain of what really happened.)

Future Modals: *Should, Ought to, May, Might,* and *Could* (Uncertainty)

Example (modal + base verb)	Rule
He ***should* report** the identity theft. (He ***shouldn't* report** the identity theft.) He ***ought to* report** the identity theft. (He ***ought not* report** the identity theft.)	We use *should* or *ought to* to give a strong suggestion. However, we are uncertain if it will happen.
They ***may/might/could* check** his credit information once a month. (They ***may/might/could* not check** his credit information once a month.)	We use *may, might,* and *could* to show uncertainty about what will happen in the future. *May* is more certain than *might* or *could*.

Future Continuous

Example	Rule
We **will be working** on the budget **when the financial planner arrives.**	to show when an action (simple present) interrupts a continuous action in the future (future continuous)
At 8:00 a.m. we **will be working** on the budget.	to express an action at a specific time in the future—an action that started before that time
We **will be working** on the budget while **you are talking** on the phone.	to show when two continuous actions will be happening at the same time in the future

Note: The future tense cannot be used in clauses. Therefore in the first example, we use the simple present and in the third example, we use the present continuous.

Causative Verbs: *Get, Have, Help, Make, Let*			
Subject	Verb	Noun / Pronoun (object)	Infinitive (omit *to* except for *get*)
He	will get	his handyman	to come.
She	had	her mom	wait for the repairperson.
The landlord	helped	me	move in.
Melanie	makes	her sister	pay half of the rent.
Mr. Martin	let	Melanie	skip one month's rent.

• Transitive verbs are verbs that require a direct object. Causative verbs are usually transitive verbs.

Perception Verbs		
Subject + verb	Direct object	Gerund or Base
Simple Present		
I see / watch / look at	the landlord	fixing the sink.
I notice / observe	the gardener	clipping bushes on Tuesday.
I feel	the light switch in the dark.	
I hear / listen to	music	filling the room.
I smell	a strange odor.	
Simple Past		
I saw / watched / looked at	my neighbor	water (watering) the plants.
I noticed / observed	everything that went on there.	
I felt	the cold water	run (running).
I heard / listened to	noises	come (coming) from upstairs.
I smelled	a sweet smell.	

• Transitive verbs require a direct object. Perception verbs are usually transitive verbs.
• In the present tense, use the gerund if needed after the direct object. **Note:** In most of the examples above, the gerund is not needed. It just adds more information.
• In the past tense, use the base or gerund after the direct object.

Comparative and Superlative Adjectives			
Type of adjective	**Simple form**	**Comparative form**	**Superlative form**
One-syllable adjectives	high	**higher**	**the highest**
One-syllable adjectives that end in **-e**	nice	**nicer**	**the nicest**
One-syllable adjectives that end in *consonant-vowel-consonant*	big	**bigger**	**the biggest**
Two-syllable adjectives that end in **-y**	pricey	**pricier**	**the priciest**
Other two-syllable adjectives	decent	**more decent**	**the most decent**
Some two-syllable adjectives have two forms	quiet friendly	**quieter** *or* **more quiet** **friendlier** *or* **more friendly**	**the quietest** *or* **the most quiet** **the friendliest** or **the most friendly**
Adjectives with three or more syllables	expensive	**more expensive**	**the most expensive**

- Use the comparative form to compare two things.
- If the second item is expressed, use *than*.
    My apartment is **bigger than** hers.
- Use the superlative form to compare one thing to two or more things.
- A prepositional phrase is sometimes used at the end of a superlative sentence.
    My automobile mechanic is the nicest repairman **in the business**.

	Simple Form	**Comparative Form**	**Superlative Form**
Irregular Adjectives	good bad far little much/many	better worse farther less more	the best the worst the farthest the least the most
Irregular Adverbs	well badly a little a lot	better worse less more	the best the worst the least the most

Adverbial Clauses of Time		
Main clause (independent clause)	**Subordinate conjunction**	**Subordinate clause (dependent clause)**
I spoke to you	after	you examined me on Friday.
Don't pay anything	before	you get an itemized bill.
She felt sicker	when	she saw the bill.
He made the co-pay	while	she was being examined.
We'll send your bill	as soon as	your insurance pays their portion.
She explained the situation	once	the patient calmed down.
• The time clause can also go first and is followed by a comma.		
After you called me on Friday, I spoke to you. While she was being examined, he made the co-pay.		
• Subordinate adverbial clauses have a subject and verb construction, but are dependent on the main clause for their meaning.		

Adverbial Clauses of Reason		
Main clause	**Subordinate conjunction**	**Subordinate clause (dependent clause)**
Health insurance is important	because	you never know when there might be an emergency.
The insurance paid the bill	since	we paid all the premiums on time.
The insurance questioned the charges	as	we had quite a few visits in one month.
You can get hip surgery	now that	you have health insurance.
He will keep the PPO	as long as	the premiums don't get too expensive.
• The reason clause can also go first and is followed by a comma.		
Since we paid all the premiums on time, the insurance paid. As long as the premiums don't get too expensive, we will keep the PPO.		
• Subordinate adverbial clauses have a subject and verb construction, but are dependent on the main clause for their meaning. Adverbial clauses of reason tell why something happens or is done.		

Adverbial Clauses of Concession		
Main clause	**Subordinate conjunction**	**Subordinate clause (dependent clause)**
He says he doesn't have a gambling problem	although	he spends a lot of time in Vegas.
She tries to stop eating so much	though	she still eats over 4000 calories a day.
He smokes 3 packs of cigarettes a day	even though	he says he is quitting.
We are good students	in spite of the fact that	we are addicted to shopping.
The doctor said to take the medicine	even if	I don't like the taste.
* *though* is the same as *although* but less formal. *Even though* shows a stronger contrast.		
• The clause of concession can always go first and is offset from the main clause by a comma.		
Although he spends a lot of time in Vegas, he says he doesn't have a gambling problem. Even though he says he is quitting, he smokes 3 packs of cigarettes a day.		
• Subordinate adverbial clauses have a subject and verb construction, but are dependent on the main clause for their meaning. Adverbial clauses of concession show a contrast to the main clause.		

Adverbial Clauses of Condition 1			
Main clause	**Subordinate conjunction**	**Subordinate clause (dependent clause)**	
The doctor will be unhappy	if	you don't take your medication.	
She will be on time for her appointment	unless	the bus is late.	has the opposite meaning of *if*
They will be on time for the appointment	provided that	the bus is on time.	has a similar meaning to *if*
He will get better	only if	he follows the doctor's instructions.	more definite than *if*
• The clause of condition can always go first and is offset from the main clause by a comma.			
If you don't take your medicine, the doctor will not be happy.			
• Subordinate adverbial clauses have a subject and verb construction, but are dependent on the main clause for their meaning. Adverbial clauses of condition show the circumstances when the main clause is true.			

Adverbial Clauses of Condition 2

Main clause	Subordinate conjunction	Subordinate clause (dependent clause)
You should take an aspirin a day	whether or not	you have any chest pains.
You should always be prepared	in case	there is an emergency.
You should get a second opinion	even if	you are satisfied with the first.

• The clause of condition can always go first and is offset from the main clause by a comma.

Even if you are satisfied with the first opinion, you should get a second.

• Subordinate adverbial clauses have a subject and verb construction, but are dependent on the main clause for their meaning. Adverbial clauses of condition show the circumstances when the main clause is true.

Adjective Clauses That Modify Indefinite Pronouns

Person (who)	She is someone *who sells her fair share of cars*. Anybody *who shops like he does* must have a lot of money.
Thing (*that* or *which*)	Everything *(that) they bought* had to be returned. Anything *that glowed* she wanted to have.

Indefinite pronouns are pronouns that are not specific like *someone* and *anything*.
Indefinite pronouns include:

   another, anyone, anybody, anything, everyone, everybody, everything, nothing, each, either, no one, neither, nobody, one, someone, somebody, something, both, few, many, several

Adjective Clauses with Subject Pronouns

	Adjective clause	Clause construction
Person (*whom*)	She is the salesperson *who was in the store yesterday.* The salesperson *who was in the store yesterday* was excellent. (*Who* is the subject of the adjective clauses and modifies the preceding noun.)	relative pronoun + **verb** who + was
Thing (*that* or *which*)	They bought the patio furniture *that was on sale*. The furniture *which is on sale* is beautiful. (*That* and *which* are the subject of the adjective clauses and modify the preceding noun.)	that + was which + is

• Restrictive adjective clauses give essential information.
    They bought the patio furniture *that was on sale*. This means there was some furniture that wasn't
    on sale and the clause specifies only the furniture on sale.

• Nonrestrictive adjective clauses give extra unnecessary information. Use commas to offset
 the clause and use *which* not *that* for things.
    They bought the patio furniture, *which was on sale*. This means all the furniture was on sale
    and the information was not necessary to distinguish it from other furniture.

Adjective Clauses Using *When*, *Where*, or *Why*

	Adjective clause	Clause construction		
		relative adverb +	**subject** +	**verb**
Place	The store *where we bought the furniture* didn't offer a product guarantee. We bought a new guitar at a store *where they don't offer service guarantees*.	where	we	bought
		where	they	don't offer
Time	We bought the computer on the day *when they were offering extended warranties*. She never thought she'd see the day *when you could buy things on the internet*.	when	they	were offering
		when	you	could buy
Reason	The reason *why they didn't buy the printer* is it printed too slowly. Slow service is the reason *why we never shop at that store*.	why	they	didn't buy
		why	we	never shop

All adjective clauses have three essential components: 1. They contain a subject and a verb; 2. They begin with either a relative pronoun, *who, whom, whose, that* or *which*; or a relative adverb, *where, when,* or *why*; and 3. They function as an adjective.

Adjective Clauses with *Whose*

Replacing a possessive adjective	Clause construction
I want to buy a cat. *Its* lineage should be purebred. **Converts to:** I want to buy a cat *whose* lineage is purebred.	*Whose* replaces a *possessive adjective* that precedes a person or a thing. It refers to both animate and inanimate nouns.
Robert bought a new TV. *His* old TV was broken. **Converts to:** Robert, *whose* old TV was broken, bought a new one.	
The family just moved in. *Their* house is for sale. **Converts to:** The family *whose* house is for sale just moved in.	*whose* + noun + verb

- The rule for restrictive and nonrestrictive clauses applies to these adjective clauses as well. When the clause is necessary for clarity, no commas are used to offset it.

Nouns: Phrases, Pronouns, Clauses

Definition	Example sentences
Pronouns: words that take the place of nouns including subject pronouns, object pronouns, possessive pronouns, and reflexive pronouns.	*It* is difficult. (subject) Javier loves *it*. (object) His computer is over there next to *mine*. (possessive) She sees *herself* in an office job in two years. (reflexive)
Noun phrase: a group of words with a noun as the main word.	*His job* is difficult. They need *three computers* for *the office*.
Noun clause: A group of words that have a subject and verb. The clause may function as a noun. It can be the subject or object of a sentence.	*What he does* is difficult. (subject) He loves *what he does*. (object)

Noun Clauses as Objects of Prepositions

	Preposition	Noun clause = object of the preposition
We are concerned	about	*what* she needs to do.
I am interested	in	*what* you have to say.
We can't decide	on	*who* we want for the new supervisor.
We went	to	*where* the paper was stored.
I spoke	about	*how* he treated other employees.

• A noun clause as the object of a preposition starts with a question word and is followed by a subject and verb.

Noun Clauses as Complements

Subject	Verb	Noun clause = Complement	Clause construction
It	seems	*that they work together well as a team.*	
They	are	*what we would call well-organized.*	*that* + subject + verb
She	became	*what they considered a problem in the office.*	
He	got	*what he wanted.*	*what* + subject + verb
You	felt	*what I said had merit, didn't you?*	

A complement always follows "to be", "to become", "to get", "to feel", or "to seem."

Noun Clauses as Subjects

Noun clause = Subject	Verb	
That our whole department got a raise	was	a surprise to us.
What we did yesterday	made	a big difference in office efficiency.
How she did her job	benefited	everyone.
Where I went	is	none of your business.
How they spoke to us	helped	me understand my job.

• A noun clause as a subject of the verb starts with a question word or *that* and is followed by a subject and verb.

Noun Clauses as Objects of Verbs

Subject + Verb	Noun clause	Explanation
I did	*what* I was asked.	• A noun clause as an object of the verb starts with a question word or *that* and is followed by a subject and verb. • In this case, the noun clauses are the object of the sentence.
She knows	*how* to do a PowerPoint presentation.	
They decided	*where* the location would be.	
My boss asked	*who* would be best for the job.	
I hope	*that* they worked as a team.	

Noun Clauses with *Whether* and *If*

Expression	*whether/if*	Clause
I don't know	*if*	we will keep our jobs (or not).
I wanted to know	*whether*	(or not) we would work Monday.
We discussed	*if*	he would continue with the project (or not).

• Use *whether* or *if* for statements where there is doubt to something being true or false. Using *or not* is optional but falls in a different place depending on which word you use. Either word can be used.
• *Whether* and *if* statements are sometimes considered embedded questions. Consider the following:

Will we keep our jobs?	I don't know if we will keep our jobs.
Would we work tomorrow?	I wanted to know whether we will work Monday.
Would he continue?	We discussed if he would continue.

Articles: *A, An,* and *The*

Rules (article + noun)	Example	What it means
a or ***an*** Use *a* or *an* when the noun that follows represents one of a class of things or when the sentence is making a generalization. *An* is used when the noun that follows starts with a vowel sound.	*A citizen* has specific rights.	a citizen = any citizen or just citizens in general; sometimes the speaker means all citizens
the Use *the* when the listener and the speaker both have the same specific idea in mind represented by the noun.	*The citizen* we spoke about yesterday has his rights.	the citizen = a specific person who has already been identified

Note: Singular count nouns must be preceded by an article, *this/that*, or a possessive adjective.

Definite Articles *vs.* Nothing		
Rules (article + noun)	**Example**	**What it means**
the Use *the* when the listener and the speaker both have the same specific idea in mind represented by the noun.	***The** rights* that citizens have include the right to vote.	the rights = specific rights outlined in the U.S. Constitution
ø Use no article with plural nouns when making generalizations.	*Citizens* have specific rights.	citizens = any citizen or just citizens in general; sometimes the speaker means all citizens
ø Use no article with noncount nouns when making generalizations.	*Justice* is another word for *fairness* under the law.	justice and fairness = generalizations that cannot be counted
ø Use no article with proper names unless the article is part of the name (The United States of America.)	*Judge Harvey Spanner* declared his support for the new mayor.	Judge Harvey Spanner = the name of the judge
Note: Singular count nouns must be preceded by an article, *this/that*, or a possessive adjective.		

Demonstrative Determiners and Pronouns		
	Singular	**Plural**
Near	*this*	*these*
Far	*that*	*those*
Demonstratives determiners (or *adjectives*) tell the reader if the noun is near or far and singular or plural. *Demonstrative pronouns* represent a noun that is near or far and singular or plural. Nouns can be omitted if referred to previously.		
	Examples	
Near (space)	*This* (trash can) is used for recycling.	The trash can is near the speaker.
Far (space)	*That* (trash can) is used for recycling.	The trash can is not within reaching distance of the speaker.
Near (time)	*These* (recycling systems) we learned about are great.	They learned about the recycling system a short time ago, probably the same day.
Far (time)	*Those* (recycling systems) we learned about are great.	They learned about the recycling system previously.

Such and Demonstrative Determiners

Determiner	Example	Explanation
this + noun Use *this* with singular nouns that represent specific things.	Her opinion is that we should all carpool. Is *this* opinion really based on reality?	*This* refers to the specific opinion that everyone should carpool.
such a(n) + noun Use *such a* with singular nouns that represent classes or subgroups of the nouns.	Her opinion is that we should all carpool. Is *such an* opinion really based on reality?	*Such an* is referring to any opinion like the one mentioned and not only the opinion that everyone should carpool.
these + noun Use *these* with plural nouns that represent specific things.	Carpool lanes with walls on either side can be dangerous in accidents. *These* lanes are difficult to merge in and out of.	*These* lanes refers only to the specific carpool lanes with walls on either side.
such + noun Use *such* with plural nouns that represent classes or groups that have been specified.	Carpool lanes with walls on either side can be dangerous in accidents. *Such* lanes are also difficult to merge in and out of.	*Such* lanes refers to all of those carpool lanes with walls on either side.
Use *this* or *such* with noncount nouns. Use *this* for specific and *such* for general.		

Contrary-to-Fact Conditionals: Statements

Condition (*if* + subject + past tense verb)	Result (subject + *would* + base verb)
If I had a million dollars, **If you didn't have** so much work, **If she were** a smart consumer, **If I weren't** busy,	**I would buy** a new house. **you would take** a long vacation. **she would read** sales ads carefully. **I would shop** around.

- A contrary-to-fact statement is a sentence that is not true at this point in time.
- A comma is used between the two clauses when the *if*-clause comes first.
- The *if*-clause can come first or second. When it comes second, no comma is used.
    I would buy a new house **if I had** a million dollars.
- In the *if*-clause, use *were* instead of *was* with *I, he, she,* and *it.*

Contrary-to-fact Conditionals: *Yes/No* Questions

if + subject + past tense / *would* + subject + base verb	Short answer	
If you had more money, **would you buy** a car? **If he didn't have** so much work, **would he take** a vacation? **If they weren't** busy, **would they shop** around?	Yes, **I would.** Yes, he **would.** Yes, they **would.**	No, I **wouldn't.** No, he **wouldn't.** No, they **wouldn't.**

- A *yes/no* question in a contrary-to-fact conditional is formed in the result clause.
- The *if*-clause can come first or second. When it comes second, no comma is used.
    Would you buy a car **if you had** more money?

PHOTO CREDITS